THE
LAST DAYS OF
IMPERIAL
RUSSIA

THE
LAST DAYS OF
IMPERIAL
RUSSIA

Miriam Kochan

Macmillan Publishing Co., Inc.
New York

To Nick, Anna, Benjy
and their father

Macmillan Publishing Co., Inc.
866 Third Avenue, New York, N.Y. 10022

Library of Congress Cataloging in Publication Data

Kochan, Miriam.
 The last days of imperial Russia, 1910–1914.

 Includes index.
 1. Russia–History–1904–1914. 2. Russia–Social
conditions. I. Title.
DK262.K63 1976 947.08 76–12437
ISBN 0–02–564900–0

First American Edition 1976

Printed in Great Britain.

CONTENTS

INTRODUCTION

In March 1917 the last Romanov Tsar was forced to abdicate. Imperial Russia, which had existed as a powerful, violent, colourful entity for 300 years, was consigned to history.

Over the years, as Romanov Tsar succeeded Romanov Tsar, the wild, vast, Asiatic country had become a European state and a world power. But the sharp divisions which marked it remained. In 1914 the country was still governed by an all-powerful Tsar, his absolute power little limited by minor concessions to modern democratic formulas. There was still a very small rich and influential class enjoying privileges unknown and unconceived of by the vast masses of the country's poor, who lived in a state of degradation not experienced elsewhere in the West for many centuries. The atmosphere was still pervaded by a quality of potential violence which had exploded on and off throughout the 300 years of Romanov rule. Tsars had been murdered by their subjects or by rivals for the throne. Revolt had more than once seriously threatened the Empire. Why then did the revolution of February 1917 succeed in destroying this mighty structure which had withstood so many centuries of assault?

Some lay the blame on the character of the Tsar—autocrat currently seated on the throne, Nicholas Romanov. Others place responsibility squarely on the shoulders of his wife, the Empress Alexandra Feodorovna. Still others attribute the collapse of the regime to the 'man of God' Gregory Rasputin. There are even attempts to relate the breakdown of an Empire to the faulty gene which caused the heir to the throne, the Tsarevich Alexis, to suffer from haemophilia.

Few subjects have been so heavily analysed by participants, historians and novelists, and few have produced so much literature directed towards exonerating one party and placing guilt on another. Through this wilderness of bias I have tried to cut a precarious middle way, and to depict objectively life and society during the last months of imperial Russia's glory, before she succumbed to war and revolution.   M.L.K.

1 The Seeds of Revolt

Astrange sight greeted the visitor to the Winter Palace in St Petersburg on 27 April 1906. The motley collection of individuals who crowded the throne room of the magnificent building which the Italian architect Rastrelli had built for the Empress Elizabeth on the banks of the Neva, and which Catherine the Great had embellished to her own taste, bore little resemblance to its normal noble inhabitants. Eleven years later, the Palace would witness still stranger scenes.

The St George's Salon, with the throne at one end against a background of the imperial coat of arms embroidered in gold on red velvet, with its white marble Corinthian pillars and its six beautiful chandeliers 'presented a queer spectacle at this moment', wrote Count Kokovtsov, Minister of Finance to the Tsar, 'and I believe its walls had never before witnessed such a scene. The entire right side of the room was filled with uniformed people, members of the State Council, and, farther on, the Tsar's retinue.' But it was the left side of the room on which all eyes were focused. It was

crowded with the members of the Duma, a small number of whom had appeared in full dress, while the overwhelming majority, occupying the first places near the throne, were dressed as if intentionally in workers' blouses and cotton shirts, and behind them was a crowd of peasants in the most varied costumes, some in national dress, and a multitude of representatives of the clergy. The first place among these representatives of the people was occupied by a man of tall stature, dressed in a worker's blouse and high oiled boots, who examined the throne and those about it with a derisive and insolent air. . . .

The slim figure of Tsar Nicholas II, flanked by his family, stood by the throne. Clearly and distinctly he read the speech inaugurating Russia's first elected parliament.

It was a painful moment for many of those present. The Dowager Empress Marie Feodorovna, the Tsar's mother, could hardly restrain her tears. 'I could not stop myself looking at certain faces', she told Kokovtsov later, 'so much did they seem to reflect an incomprehensible hatred for us all.'

'The deputies?' Count Fredericks, Minister of the Court, said to A. A. Mossolov, head of the Court Chancellery. 'They give me the impression of a gang of criminals who are only waiting for the signal to throw themselves upon the Ministers and cut their throats. What wicked faces!'

PREVIOUS PAGES Workers on strike at the Lysva metal works, Perm.

ABOVE The imperial family arrive at the Winter Palace for the opening of the first Duma, April 1906.

RIGHT The façade of the Winter Palace, a photograph taken by the Tsarina.

The magnificent throne room of the Winter Palace, the setting for the 1906 Duma. Painting by Edward Gow.

Caught in the camera eye of personal reminiscences, all the forces which dominated the last days of imperial Russia are present in this cameo. Against the sumptuous background of the Winter Palace, the Tsar's official residence, the epitome of imperial splendour, are gathered the representatives of the Russian masses, the workers and peasants, breathing antagonism to the power of the autocracy. Facing them is the very symbol of autocracy, the Tsar, surrounded by the imperial family and his ministers, radiating fear of the unleashed forces of democracy. The protagonists were in position. The atmosphere was charged with emotion. The scene was set for revolution. . . .

In fact, the seeds of revolution had long been inherent in the Russian system. At the end of the nineteenth century, Russia's vast expanses still contained extremes of poverty and wealth which had been unknown for centuries elsewhere in the West. A small noble minority owned most of the power and a large portion of the wealth. A vast peasant majority, despite the 1861 decree of emancipation which had changed them from serfs into 'free' men, lived in conditions of indescribable penury and squalor. A small group of students, disaffected nobility and professional men – the intelligentsia – who, since the days of Catherine the Great, had challenged the existing order, was an ever-present source of ferment. Over them all ruled the Tsar: an autocrat, with absolute power, assisted in the task of government by ministers whom he himself selected in conjunction with a Council of State, nomination to which he controlled.

This potentially inflammable situation had been aggravated by a massive programme of industrialization which created a new and disruptive stratum of society – an industrial proletariat. Russian industry had, in fact, been developing since the Crimean War of 1854–6, and had been given a further impetus by the emancipation of the serfs. But it still lagged immeasurably behind the West, and in the 1890s, under the leadership of Count Serge Yulievich Witte, the outstanding spokesman of the period, the State gave its wholehearted encouragement to a programme of industrialization, in a compulsive effort to put an end to Russia's backwardness.

The statesman Count Witte, under whose influence a programme of rapid industrialization was begun in the 1890s.

Inspired by Witte's vision of Russia as a great power, and utilizing massive injections of foreign loans and investments, government subsidies and protectionist tariffs, the programme was an undoubted success: Russia's heavy industry expanded out of all recognition and the decade of the 1890s marked the juncture when Russia began to develop economically. But the passage to economic maturity brought with it the troubled adolescent problem of an increase in the urban proletariat. In other words, it created a group which hitherto had had no significance in the Russian social structure. Russian society was rigidly divided into three classes – nobility, merchants and peasants. There was no place in it for this new element. As a result, the new stratum, poverty-stricken, uprooted from the countryside, unprotected, provided malleable material for that other disinherited faction – the intelligentsia. With no place in the social structure, these two sectors were inevitably forced into opposition to the regime. The all-absorbing question, as Russia entered the twentieth century, was whether the old system was going to prove flexible enough to absorb the new

Scenes of heavy
industry like this,
though common in
most countries of
western Europe, were
a comparatively recent
innovation in Russia
at this time.

pressures in time to prevent its violent overthrow and replacement by a new order.

In August 1904 the French Ambassador, Monsieur Bompard,
gave his impressions of the Russian social scene after a year or so
in St Petersburg: 'All classes of Russian society', he wrote, 'are
in a state of effervescence.' The peasants were 'a ready prey' for
agitators. The proletariat, though of recent origin, had shown
itself revolutionary from the outset; it expressed its claims 'in
the most violent forms'. Schools and universities were 'seed-
beds of anarchists'. Students applauded terrorist attacks, and
some participated in them. The merchant class, save for some
honourable exceptions, was composed of 'rapacious and un-
scrupulous hawkers'. The nobility were '*frondeurs*, blunderers
and devoid of practical sense'. The bureaucracy was 'a scourge',
the ministers were progressively more mediocre and the Tsar
clung to an authority 'that he was incapable of exercising'.

The last years of the old century and the first years of the
new one did indeed see gathering symptoms of unrest. There
were continual strikes among workers at the industrial plants.

Peasant disorders in the countryside became a common feature. Dramatic assassination attempts were made by students against prominent members of the government. Despite a ban on the formation of political parties, three actually came into being among the intelligentsia: the Social Revolutionaries, who believed in revolution led by peasants; a liberal party, anxious for constitutional government; and the Social Democrats, who favoured revolution by the working class.

Nor was the right wing totally inactive. A reactionary group, blindly supporting the autocracy, was already in existence (some said with Tsarist support) in the Union of the Russian People, popularly referred to as 'The Black Hundreds'. One of its most potent weapons was the pogrom against the Jewish population of the country. In 1903, one such attack was viciously unleashed in an attempt to divert public attention from the basic internal state of discontent.

In the midst of these upheavals, in January 1904, Russia embarked on an irrelevant and, in the event, wholly abortive war with Japan. Viacheslav Konstantinovich Plehve, Minister of the Interior, had said that 'in order to hold back the revolution, we need a small victorious war'. War did not, on this occasion, constitute the universal panacea. It did not bind the disunited people of Russia together into one coherent, patriotic body. On the contrary, it brought to the fore all the discordant forces which until then had remained peripheral. The assassinations by revolutionary groups continued. On 15 July 1905 Plehve, himself a symbol (possibly erroneously) of the government's policy of repression, its contempt for public opinion, anti-semitism and bureaucratic tyranny, was killed by a Social Revolutionary bomb. Dr Dillon, the *Daily Telegraph* correspondent, happened to be passing when

. . . two men on bicycles glided past, followed by a closed carriage, which I recognized as that of the all-powerful minister. Suddenly, the ground before me quivered, a tremendous sound as of thunder deafened me, the windows of the houses on both sides of the broad street rattled and the glass of the panes was hurled on to the stone pavements. A dead horse, a pool of blood, fragments of a carriage, and a hole in the ground were parts of my rapid impression. My driver was on his knees devoutly praying and saying that the end of the world had come. . . . Plehve's end was received with semi-public rejoicings. I met nobody who regretted his assassination or condemned the authors.

Matters moved rapidly to a climax. In an atmosphere of widespread unrest, aggravated by worsening war news, a massive strike broke out in the Putilov metal works, the largest industrial concern in St Petersburg, which employed some 10,000 workers. It was led by a priest, Father George Gapon, who had organized an Association of Factory and Mill Workers with the connivance of the police (who had hoped thereby to remove control of workers' movements from the hands of the revolutionaries). This, in fact, was a typical ploy of the Okhrana, the secret police. In an attempt to maintain order within the State, Okhrana agents had infiltrated everywhere: they were in the army, in schools, within political organizations, clubs, secret revolutionary societies – and among the workers. They kept under surveillance not only people who might be suspected of subversive activities but anyone who might arouse the curiosity of the Police Director or his minions. Witte reports that even the

Workers at the
huge Putilov metal works
in St Petersburg,
January 1905.

letters of the Dowager Empress were opened, while he himself had to write his memoirs abroad to escape their clutches.

The strike at the Putilov plant spread, and Gapon was persuaded to lead a mass demonstration to the Winter Palace to carry a petition to the Tsar.

O Sire [they addressed the Tsar], we working men of St Petersburg, our wives and children, and our parents, helpless and aged men and women, have come to you, our ruler, in quest of justice and protection. We are beggars, we are oppressed and overburdened with work; we are insulted, we are not regarded as human beings but are treated as slaves who must suffer their bitter lot in silence. We have suffered but are driven further and further into the abyss of poverty, injustice and ignorance; we are strangled by despotism and tyranny, so that we can breathe no longer. We have no strength at all, Sovereign. Our patience is at an end. We are approaching that terrible moment when death is better than the continuance of intolerable sufferings. . . .

Our first wish was to discuss our needs with our employers, but this was refused to us: we were told that we have no legal right to discuss our conditions. We were told also that it is illegal to insist on the eight-hour day and on the fixing of wage-rates in consultation with us. We were not allowed to discuss our complaints over the behaviour of the lower administrative staff. We asked that wages of casual labourers and women should be raised to one rouble a day, that overtime should be abolished and that more adequate medical attention should be provided for us with care and without humiliation. We asked that the factories should be rebuilt so that we could work in them without suffering from draughts, rain and snow. . . .

Your Majesty! We are here, many thousands of us; we have the appearance of human beings, but in fact we have no human rights at all, not even the right to speak, to think, or to meet for discussion of our requirements on the steps to be taken for the improvement of our conditions. We are turned into slaves by your officials. Any one of us who dares to raise his voice in defence of the working class is thrown into prison, sent into exile. The mere fact of having a kind heart or a sensitive soul is regarded as a crime; to show sympathy with the lowly, the oppressed, the tortured is to commit a heavy crime. Every worker and peasant is at the mercy of your officials, who accept bribes, rob the Treasury and do not care at all for the people's interests. The bureaucracy of the government has ruined the country, involved it in a shameful war and is leading Russia nearer and nearer to utter ruin. We, the Russian workers and people, have no voice at all in the expenditure of the huge sums collected in taxes from the impoverished population. We do not even know how our money is spent. The people are deprived of any right to discuss taxes and their expenditure. The workers have no right to organize their own labour unions for the defence of their own interests.

Is this, O Sovereign, in accordance with the laws of God, by whose grace you reign? And how can we live under such laws? Break down the wall between yourself and your people. . . . The people must be represented in the control of the country's affairs. Only the people themselves know their own needs. Do not reject their help, accept it, command forthwith that representatives of all classes, groups, professions and trades shall come together. Let capitalists and workers, bureaucrats and priests, doctors and teachers, meet together and choose their representatives. Let all be equal and free. And to this end let the election of members to the Constituent Assembly take place in conditions of universal, secret and equal suffrage. . . .

Everything was done to order. The police and members of the government were warned of the event beforehand, and it was a totally peaceful procession led by the handsome, bearded peasant–priest which moved across the snow on 9 January 1905. The people wore their Sunday best. They were singing hymns and carrying ikons, as well as portraits of the Tsar. Totally unexpected was the attack which suddenly broke upon them. Before the orderly throng could hand their petition to the Tsar, before they had even reached the Winter Palace Square, a horde of Cossack cavalry charged into their midst. An infantry regiment followed, shooting into the crowd. The people – those who were able – scattered in terror. All that remained of that peaceful Sunday morning scene were the bodies of those trampled or shot, scarring the pure white of the snow. Count Witte, watching from his balcony, saw

. . . a dense crowd moving along the Kamenoostrovski Prospect. These people included many intellectuals, women and children. Before ten minutes had passed, shots sounded in the direction of the Troitzky Bridge. A bullet whistled by close to me; another killed the doorman at the Alexander *Lycée*. The last thing I saw was a large number of wounded being carried away in carriages, a crowd running in disarray, with here and there women weeping. . . .

The official casualty list for 'Bloody Sunday' noted 130 dead. The actual figure was probably much higher. Its effects were immeasurable. Horror at the massacre released all the pent-up violence within the Russian nation. The country was hit as

Dazed and mutilated, the Bloody Sunday demonstrators stagger away from the Cossacks' sabre charge. An artist's impression drawn for *The Illustrated London News*, but probably very close to the truth.

OVERLEAF With cool precision, the infantry line up awaiting their officer's order to shoot the fleeing survivors.

19

never before by a wave of strikes, riots and demonstrations. The universities closed their doors, and in a fresh outbreak of Social Revolutionary terrorism Grand Duke Serge, uncle of the Tsar, husband of the Tsarina Alexandra's sister, and an avowed reactionary, was murdered in a bomb attempt on 2 February 1905, as he was driving across the Moscow Kremlin. As luck would have it, his wife, Grand Duchess Elizabeth, was in the Kremlin at the time, organizing a Red Cross sewing guild to help the troops. Hearing the explosion, she rushed down into the street – in time to gather together the pieces of her husband's body which lay scattered over the snow. The bomb had caught Serge full in the chest.

His assassin, Kalayev, explained his action at his trial:

I am not a defendant here, I am your prisoner. We are two warring camps. You – the representatives of the imperial government, the hired servants of capital and oppression. I – one of the avengers of the people, a socialist and revolutionist. Mountains of corpses divide us, hundreds of thousands of broken human lives and a whole sea of blood and tears covering the country in torrents of horror and resentment. You have declared war upon the people. We have accepted your challenge. Having taken me prisoner, it is now within your power to subject me to the torture of slow extinction or to kill me outright, but you cannot hold trial over me. No matter how much you may seek to exercise your sway, there can be no justification for you as there can be no condemnation of me. Between you and me there can be no reconciliation, as it cannot be between absolutism and the people. We are still the same enemies, and if, having deprived me of liberty and the opportunity to speak directly to the people, you have seen fit to institute this solemn judgment upon me, I am in no way obliged to recognize you as my judges. . . . Let us be tried by this great martyr of history – the Russia of the people.

Terrified by the uncontrolled violence within his country, overwhelmed by the demands made upon him, Tsar Nicholas agreed to allow a representative assembly to meet in a consultative capacity. But his concession came too late and was too meagre. It was met by a united front of the forces of opposition to the regime, by renewed general strikes, violence, mutinies and resistance. Fighting broke out throughout Russia. Maurice Baring, the English man of letters, noted:

The outward aspect of the town during these days is strange. Moscow seems like a besieged city. Many of the shops have got great wooden shutters. Some of the doors are marked with a large red cross. The distress, I am told, during the strike was terrible. There was no light, no gas, no water, all the shops were shut; provisions and wood were scarce. This afternoon I went to see Bauman's funeral procession [Bauman was a veterinary surgeon who had been shot during the disturbances], which I witnessed from many parts of the town. It was one of the most impressive sights I have ever seen. A hundred thousand men took part in it. The whole of the 'intelligentsia' (the professional and middle class) was in the streets or at the windows. The windows and balconies were crowded with people. Order was perfect. There was not a hitch nor a scuffle. The men walking in the procession consisted of students, doctors, workmen, people in various kinds of uniform. There were ambulances, with doctors dressed in white in them, in case there should be casualties. The men bore great red banners and the coffin was covered with a scarlet pall. As they marched they sang in a low chant the '*Marseillaise*'. . . . As it grew dark, torches were brought out, lighting up the red banners and the scarlet coffin. . . . As I saw these hundred thousand men march past so quietly, so simply, in their bourgeois clothes, singing in careless, almost conversational fashion, I seemed nevertheless to hear the 'tramping of innumerable armies'. . . .

In St Petersburg, Moscow and other large centres, workers began to organize themselves into governments of their own. Soviets (workers' councils) were formed and made a considerable impact. It seemed to many people at this point that the revolution had indeed arrived. Baring commented on a minor but nonetheless significant symptom. He went into a Moscow barber's shop and asked for a bar of soap. 'Give the *citizen* some soap', ordered the assistant, aged about ten. Outside, he found the streets decorated with flags, and everybody in a state of frantic excitement. In the restaurants, old men were embracing each other and drinking the first glass of vodka 'to Free Russia'. To cap it all at this juncture, as a final blow to the regime, the news came through that the Russian forces had been decisively defeated by the Japanese at the battle of Tsushima.

In October 1905, persuaded by Count Witte if not by the overriding force of circumstances, the Tsar capitulated and published the manifesto which allowed the first Duma to be elected. Slowly, the rioting died down. Gradually, the Soviets faded away. Russia's first Duma met.

It should not be thought that Tsar Nicholas had experienced a sudden conversion, in allowing the Duma to meet. It would

The Duma meets in the elegant surroundings of the Tauride Palace.

not even appear from his subsequent action that he was fully aware of the long-term necessity of representative government if the regime were to survive. Throughout his abbreviated reign he remained firmly opposed to all forms of liberalism. He had granted permission for the Duma under duress. He wrote to his mother at the time:

You remember, no doubt, those January days when we were together at Tsarskoe – they were miserable, weren't they? But they are *nothing* in comparison with what has happened now. . . . All sorts of conferences took place in Moscow. . . . God knows what happened in the universities. Every *kind* of riff-raff walked in from the streets, riot was loudly proclaimed – nobody seemed to mind. . . . It makes me sick to read the news! . . . But the Ministers, instead of acting with quick decision, only assemble in Council like a lot of frightened hens and cackle about providing united ministerial action. . . . Trepov made it quite plain to the populace by his proclamations that any disorder would be ruthlessly put down. . . . One had the same feeling as before a thunderstorm in summer. . . . Through all those horrible days, I constantly met Witte. We very often met in the early morning to part only in the evening when night fell. . . . There were only two ways open: to find an energetic soldier and crush the rebellion by sheer force. . . . That would mean rivers of blood, and in the end we should be where we had started. . . . The other way out would be to give to the people their civil rights, free- dom of speech and Press, also to have all laws confirmed by a State Duma – that of course, would be a constitution. Witte defends this very energetically. . . . Almost everybody I had an opportunity of consulting is of the same opinion. Witte put it quite clearly to me that he would accept the Presidency of the Council of Ministers only on the condition that his programme was agreed to, and his actions not interfered with. . . . We discussed it for two days and in the end, invoking God's help, I signed. . . . There was no other way out than to cross oneself and give what everyone was asking for. . . . We are in the midst of a revolution with an administrative apparatus entirely disorganized, and in this lies the main danger.

Once the disorders in the country were quelled, the Tsar's one thought was to regather the reins of the autocracy which he regarded as his divine heritage. One of his first steps, after peace with Japan had been signed and peace within Russia restored, was to dismiss Witte and replace him as Chairman of the Council of Ministers by a more malleable character, Ivan Logginovich Goremykin, a man who was prepared to obey the Tsar and ignore the Duma. Through their connivance, both the first and the second Duma were dissolved after only a few months' existence. Before the elections to the third Duma took place, the electoral law was revised to ensure less left-wing and more right-wing landowner representation. Consequently, the third Duma enjoyed a longer though hardly influential lease of life.

However, the significant step in Russian history that these early Dumas represented should not be underestimated. They were the first move towards the establishment of constitutional government. For the first time the autocracy of the Tsar had been limited by the legislative control of two chambers. The Dumas marked the turning-point when the country at large was called in to take a direct part in the conduct of public affairs. The movement was slow, but it ended the stagnation of centuries.

Considering how new the Russian people were to parliamentary procedure, it was amazing how quickly and soberly the Duma took on the form of a Western representative assembly. Maurice Baring was particularly struck by the respect and instantaneous obedience shown to the President. The moment he rang the bell, complete silence descended on the Chamber. 'People say', Baring comments, 'that this is because the members are new to their business and that the Duma will soon learn to be as disorderly as the House of Commons.' He was also impressed by the natural way in which members spoke, without oratory or theatrical effect. He had the good fortune to attend an early meeting:

> . . . I think it is the most interesting sight I have ever seen. When you arrive at the Tauride Palace, which outside has an appearance of dignified stateliness, the stateliness of the end of the eighteenth century, you walk through a spacious front hall into what looks like a gigantic white ballroom built in the late Louis XVI style. This is the lobby; beyond it is the Hall of the Duma itself. In this long gallery members and visitors were already flocking, walking up and down, talking and smoking cigarettes and throwing away the ashes and the ends on the polished floor. One saw peasants in their long black coats, some of them wearing military medals and crosses; popes [parish priests], Tartars, Poles, men in every kind of dress except uniform. When the sitting began, I went up into the gallery. The Hall of the Duma itself is likewise white, delicate in decoration, an essentially gentleman-like room. The sitting began about three o'clock. The members go to their appointed places, on which their cards are fixed, and the impression of diversity of dress and type becomes still stronger and more picturesque. . . . The President walked into his seat under the portrait of the Emperor, which is a rather shiny study in blue and white. . . .

The years before 1914 also saw progress in another direction. It was realized that before the great illiterate masses of Russia's population could be ready to play a genuine part in a democratic form of government, tremendous advances in education would have to be made. Although a bill to unify the entire primary education system was rejected by the State Council in 1911, a plan for the introduction of universal education to be completed by 1922 was very much in existence. As a first step towards this end, a law of 3 May 1908 decreed that all children between the age of eight and eleven should receive primary education.

The task of education at a local level was backed up valiantly by the *Zemstvos*, local councils consisting of and elected by the landed gentry. Against every form of obstacle – opposition from the central government, and inertia and indifference on the part of the masses – they succeeded in introducing an impressive range of services. Apart from anything else, according to one source, some 50,000 *Zemstvo* schools came into being in the fifteen years before 1914, employing about 80,000 teachers and catering for approximately three million pupils. Count Constantine Benckendorff, possibly a prototype of the enlightened landowner who was deeply involved with the *Zemstvo* movement (he was a member of both the District and Provincial Assemblies of the *Zemstvo*), describes a typical teacher at a *Zemstvo* school in the person of:

Constantine Phillipovich, the son of a lay reader . . . and a graduate of a teachers' college. . . . An extremely efficient teacher and rather strict disciplinarian, he was entirely devoted to his duties towards both his pupils and their parents. Although of clerical stock, he was a peasant born and bred . . . and thus he was able to adjust the conflicting interests of time spent on education by the young peasantry and the need of their parents for their labour.

His wife, who was second schoolmistress, was not at all typical. She was a product of the first educational institute of university status for women, founded in the late nineteenth century in the face of a great deal of opposition. The products of these Bestouzhev Courses in their early years were exceptionally highly educated and cultured young women from all classes of society, imbued with a passionate determination to devote their lives to the enlightenment of the peasantry. This schoolmistress was a small woman with a very quiet voice, who succeeded in infusing her lessons with a special meaning which broadened the children's vision. Though Maurice Baring's claim that the Russian peasant was an avid reader of Milton's *Paradise Lost* still seems a little bizarre, it was not as wholly improbable as may at first glance seem.

Stolypin, the instigator of a number of excellent agricultural reforms, was assassinated in 1911.

The *Zemstvos* also built hospitals, dispensaries and orphanages. They erected fireproof buildings, introduced fire insurance, imported agricultural machinery, established banks and endeavoured to instruct the peasant in modern methods of agriculture.

A genuine attempt was also being made to bolster up the regime in another, much more constructive, direction. Peter Stolypin, President of the Council of Ministers, though pursuing a stern policy towards extremists, was nonetheless prepared to work with the Duma. He was also dedicated to improving the lot of the peasantry, in whom he saw a major source of support for the government and of stability for Russia. During his period of power, he introduced a series of land reforms calculated to build up a more contented if not a prosperous peasant class, by helping the peasant to break free from the iron grip of the village commune, to claim his right to land of his own and to consolidate the dispersed strips of ground he thus acquired. The movement which ensued has been likened to the enclosure movement England experienced in the eighteenth century. It is a measure of Russia's backwardness that these events took place 200 years later. And this backwardness was, in fact, still all too evident in the methods of cultivation in use. Few peasants yet possessed iron ploughs, and levels of productivity were deplorably low, so that many peasants still had to rely on other sources to supplement their income. Furthermore, only the richest and most enterprising members of the peasantry knew how to profit from the Stolypin reforms.

Nevertheless, for all their shortcomings, the reforms did to some extent satisfy the land hunger of the Russian peasantry and did buy some years of relative rural quiescence for Russia. Assisted by a run of good harvests, the standard of living of the agricultural population undoubtedly rose. Temporarily, it would seem, the reforms had succeeded. How much more might have been achieved, had Stolypin lived to pursue his policies, is an open question. In 1911 he was assassinated.

His repressive measures towards the revolutionaries had always made him an unpopular figure. As early as 1906 there had been an unsuccessful attempt on his life when a bomb was thrown at his country house. Kokovtsov visited the scene shortly after the disaster and received a first-hand account from Stolypin himself: 'His reception room had been full of people, and many of the callers, as well as many servants, were among those killed or wounded. His small son had been hurt while playing on the upper balcony, but probably not seriously, whereas his daughter Natalia had suffered a serious leg wound; both children had already been removed to Kalmeier's Hospital accompanied by their mother. . . .'

On 1 September 1911, an attempt on his life at the Kiev Opera House succeeded. Young Galina von Meck, daughter of the railway magnate, was taken to the gala performance of Rimsky-Korsakov's opera *Czar Saltan* by her uncle:

I watched Stolypin standing between the stalls and the orchestra. He was talking to a group of people who surrounded him. . . . Then I noticed a man in a black suit, pushing his way in the direction of the Prime Minister's party – a moment later two revolver shots rang out. There was a hush, all eyes turned towards the front of the house where a man in black was jumping over the seats making for the left hand exit.

Stolypin remained erect for a while, with blood slowly seeping through his uniform. . . . The Prime Minister collapsed into his seat, but before he was hidden from my view, I saw him look to the left at the Imperial Box. The Emperor, who had retired to the back of the box during the interval, came out to see what had happened. Some people assert that when he appeared, Stolypin made the sign of the cross, blessing the Emperor, but that is not true. The Prime Minister, although badly wounded in the abdomen and liver, raised his left arm and twice gestured to the Tsar to keep out of sight. . . .

Supported by friends, Stolypin managed to walk out of the theatre, a brave effort which earned him a tremendous ovation. Then, when the whole audience began to sing the National Anthem, the curtain was raised and the performers, kneeling on the stage, joined in. The Emperor, standing at the front of his box, looked worried and sad, but showed no sign of fear. . . .

Five days later, Stolypin was dead.

Meanwhile, the strike movements had once again sprung to life after a period of relative calm. The agricultural reforms may have improved the peasant's lot, but they had done nothing to ameliorate the condition of the industrial worker whose numbers had been growing rapidly since the industrial upsurge which had begun in 1906 (from 1·8 million in 1906 to 2·5 million in the summer of 1914). In 1910 there were 222 strikes affecting 46,000 workers. The following year the number more than doubled, reaching 466 strikes and 105,110 workers. In 1912 matters took a more serious turn when some 5,000 employees

LEFT In 1912 the Lena
Goldfields workers in
Siberia came out on
strike in protest against
their unspeakable
working conditions.

ABOVE The goldfields
workers demonstrate –
the strike was put down
with great brutality
and several hundred
men were shot by the
police.

at the Lena Goldfields in Siberia struck in protest against low wages, the truck system of payment, degrading working conditions and a working day which extended from approximately five in the morning till seven at night. They held out for a month, until in desperation the police were called in. In the clash which resulted between police and strikers, 170 workers were killed and 372 wounded. Nothing similar had occurred since Bloody Sunday. Immediately, a widespread strike movement ensued, and by April some 500,000 men had struck in sympathy with the Lena Goldfields workers. Altogether in 1912 there were 2,052 strikes recorded, with some 725,491 men participating. In the elections to the fourth Duma held that year, the Bolshevik Party was beginning to show an increase in popularity.

2 Haute Société, St Petersburg

The 1914 social season was one of the most brilliant St Petersburg had ever seen, or would ever see again. The grey granite capital which Peter the Great had built on the banks of the Neva only 200 years earlier sparkled like a Christmas tree. In the week before New Year's Day the streets were full of bustle and activity. Money flowed freely as crowds filled the fashionable shops in Morskaya and Nevski: Conradi's, which sold superb confectionery; Denisov-Uralski's, specializing in jewels and carved animals of jade, amethyst, chalcedony and topaz; and Fabergé's, home of some of the most expensive and exquisite jewellery in the world and with an atmosphere of breathless opulence, was filled with aristocratic shoppers. There was not an appointment to be had at the hairdresser's shop on Morskaya where, so Meriel Buchanan, daughter of the British Ambassador, relates, one sat on blue and gold chairs and listened to the latest gossip.

The Russian aristocracy might have seen the golden age it enjoyed in the eighteenth century come and go, but it was still very much alive, living in a style unparalleled elsewhere in the world. It had lost in the days of Alexander II, the Tsar Emancipator, the right to own serfs (though this was only fifty-three years earlier), but it still employed peasant servants in numbers that made European visitors gasp. At the British Ambassador's residence in 1914 – and his was a relatively modest establishment – there were, in addition to the English butler, the footmen and the women's personal maids, an Italian chef with two or three men under him, two housemaids, kitchen maids, laundry maids and a seemingly infinite number of *moujiks* – little men in bright-coloured shirts and high boots who swept carpets, cleaned windows, fed furnaces, washed dishes and carried firewood. And this is not to mention the coachmen, stable hands and other outdoor staff. In addition, all the big houses in St Petersburg had their personal doormen, dressed in uniform, who wore a sort of bandolier, decorated with gold braid and coloured ornaments, on their heads. Even the restaurants were remarkable for the vast numbers of white-coated waiters who came running at the call of '*Tchelovyek!*' ('Man!').

Although the aristocrat had long been freed from the obligation to serve the State by taking employment in the army, navy or civil service in return for the privilege of owning land, he continued to live in the capital city, using his country estates merely as a source of income and provisions and as holiday resorts. Some of them, indeed, were never visited at all. The fabulously wealthy Prince Youssoupov was saddened to find one of his family's oldest estates at Spaskoie Selo near Moscow in a state of complete neglect. Once it had been a large palace on the edge of a forest of fir trees, standing on a height, and made even more impressive by a colonnade. Now its doors and windows had disappeared, and its ceilings had caved in. Stumps of marble columns protruded from the ground. . . . But the Youssoupovs had so many other estates that they could afford to allow one to fall into decay. One in the Caucasus, for example, stretched for 125 miles along the Caspian Sea. Crude petroleum, Prince Felix recounts, was so abundant there that the soil seemed soaked with it, and the peasants used it to grease their cart-wheels. This can be matched by the Benckendorff estate at Lysva in the Urals, which produced half the annual world output of platinum. Another large Youssoupov estate was at Rakitnoic in the district of Kursk. Here there were sugar plantations, numerous sawmills and several stock farms – the home of many a winner on the St Petersburg and Moscow racecourses.

The house the noble maintained in St Petersburg often approached the size and appearance of a palace on the banks of one of the canals which crossed the city. The Obolenskys were an exception to the general rule. They sold their neat white residence in Mohovaya and built a 'modern' block of flats in Mitninskaya, opposite the Winter Palace, to a French design. They kept a third of the block for their own use, with a separate entrance, stables for twelve horses and a big coach-house. The Youssoupovs' house on the Moika was, needless to say, of the palatial variety. Presented to Felix's great-great-grandmother by the Empress Catherine II, it was the scene of magnificent receptions when up to 2,000 guests would be served simultaneously with a hot supper in Sèvres china dishes from gold and silver vessels. When the 2,000 included members of the imperial family, they were entertained in the foyer while the remainder of the company were confined to the galleries. Not only did the palace house a small Louis XV theatre, but it was also a veritable treasure-house of works of art. Prince Felix's father's apartments, looking out on to the Moika Canal, were crowded with valuables: paintings by old masters covered the walls, while showcases bulged with miniatures, porcelains and snuff-boxes. Among his statuettes carved from precious stones were a Buddha made from a ruby matrix and a Venus from a sapphire. His study was an exact replica of an apartment in the Alhambra, with a fountain in the centre surrounded by columns, divans draped in Persian fabrics along the walls, and mosaics everywhere. The real showpiece of the residence, however, was the suite inhabited by Felix's mother. Her bedroom, hung with blue damask and furnished in inlaid rosewood, led into a *petit-salon*. The furniture here had once belonged to Marie Antoinette, and the rock-crystal chandelier had graced Madame de Pompadour's boudoir. Gold and enamelled snuff-boxes and ashtrays made of amethyst, topaz and jade with gem-encrusted gold settings lay scattered on tables or glistened in cabinets. On the walls hung paintings by Boucher, Fragonard, Watteau, Hubert Robert and Greuze.

The Francomania and general imitation of Western European customs which had swept through Russian society in the eighteenth century had receded, but it had left its mark. The aristocracy still employed English and French maids, English, French and German tutors and governesses. Alexander Iswolsky, Russian Ambassador to France, recalls that most of his contemporaries spoke foreign languages easily and that French was in current use at the imperial Court, in elegant St Petersburg society and among the provincial nobility. He himself did not remember writing to his parents in anything but French, heavily larded with Russicisms. The country houses scattered all over the vast Russian Empire also bore testimony to Western influence. Most of them had been built during the reign of Catherine the Great in neo-Gothic style; even in the most remote regions, they had the same columned façades and triangular frontons. The influence of Jean-Jacques Rousseau pervaded all of them. The *châteaux* were usually surrounded by parks which were dotted with temples, rustic hermitages, artificial ruins and statuary. Their libraries contained complete sets of the French philosophers and encyclopædists, and the English philosophers. The furniture, ornaments and costly silk and satin draperies were all imported from the West. Maurice Paléologue, French Ambassador to Russia, described a noblewoman's boudoir where he found 'eighteenth-century pictures, statuettes, china, brocade, lacquer, screens, inlaid work, chandeliers and side tables, a roomful of furniture in the clever and

The Youssoupovs' palatial residence
on the Moika Canal, presented to a member
of the family by Catherine the Great.

36

charming style which prevailed in the reign of Alexander I as a last blooming of French art'.

When the prima ballerina Mathilde Kschessinska furnished her new home, she ordered from Paris all the bronze pieces, such as chandeliers, brackets and candelabra, door and window handles, locks and window fastenings, as well as the carpets and furniture fabrics for her main drawing-room in Russian Empire style and her smaller drawing-room in Louis XVI style. Fashion, too, followed the Parisian lead, and the great ladies of the land received one another in their luxurious salons in gowns which would have done credit to the Rue de Rivoli – if they had not in fact originated there in the first place. For this society was accustomed to take off once or twice a year to seek a change of scene in London or Paris, Biarritz or Cannes, Rome or Venice, Baden-Baden, Karlsbad or St Moritz – and came back re-equipped with clothes, jewels, perfumes, furniture and works of literature and art. There was a whole Russian colony at Biarritz. Many of them actually owned villas there and spent several months of the year enjoying the pleasures of Biarritz social life. Others, like Nathalie Majolier, Grand Duke Michael's step-daughter, were content to rent a whole floor of a fashionable hotel for their continental holidays.

The prima ballerina Mathilde Kschessinska was Tsar Nicholas II's mistress before his marriage, and lived in magnificent style.

St Petersburg society revolved around the Court, the guards and the government, staunchly backed up by the aristocracy, whether rich or poor. Qualification for admittance was judged by birth rather than success, though leading ballet dancers, opera singers, writers, musicians and other artists were permitted to hover on the bohemian fringes. Had not the prima ballerina, Mathilde Kschessinska, been the mistress of Tsar Nicholas himself before he ascended the throne and before she formed a more permanent attachment to the man she later married, Grand Duke Andrei Vladimirovich (who was himself the Tsar's cousin)? The nobility was not, in fact, a uniform group. It embraced the old hereditary aristocrats as well as the new nobility – men who had entered State service and risen in its ranks until they attained the grades which carried with them automatic noble status under a system introduced by Peter the Great.

Haute société centred, of course, round the many members of the imperial family. The lead was taken by the Grand Duchess Marie Pavlovna. Officially she was only the third lady in the land, coming after the Empress Alexandra and the Tsar's mother, the Dowager Empress Marie Feodorovna, but as

The Grand Duchess
Marie Pavlovna,
leading light of St
Petersburg society, in
traditional Russian
costume for a ball.

Alexandra hated all public functions and had more or less withdrawn from society by 1914, and as the Dowager Empress rarely
entertained herself, Marie Pavlovna had become the virtual
leader of St Petersburg society. All the smart cosmopolitan set
followed her lead, and she entertained frequently in the spacious
white and gold rooms of her large brown palace, built in Floren-
tine style in 1870 with a façade facing the Neva. The widow of
the Tsar's uncle, the Grand Duke Vladimir, in 1907 she had
inherited his position as President of the Academy of Fine Arts,
and all the leading artists had access to her Court and came into
contact with her vivid personality and fearless strong character.

True, some of the older members of the aristocracy said that her parties were fast and vulgar, that they lacked all dignity and restraint, and that she exercised a bad influence on society generally. It was true, too, that she was accused of patronizing foreigners too freely (but she herself had been born a German princess), of inviting people because they were rich or could play bridge well, of liking to be amused and entertained – in other words, of not choosing her friends too carefully. Nonetheless, her invitations were rarely refused.

Everyone who was anyone at all, or who wanted to be, went to Marie Pavlovna's great bazaar just before Christmas, which marked the beginning of the St Petersburg season. All the leading members of society had stalls at the bazaar grouped round the central stall run by the Grand Duchess. For four days, between two o'clock and midnight the vast Hall of the Nobles resounded to the rustle of fine silks and the chatter of a hundred voices exchanging the latest gossip as the ladies

The magnificent
eighteenth-century
Anitchkov Palace, home
of the Tsar's mother,
the Dowager Empress
Marie Feodorovna.

bought expensive trifles and compared notes on each other's clothes. Aspirants to social eminence would cluster round Marie Pavlovna on these occasions. If their donations were generous enough, they could hope to be rewarded with an invitation to a reception at her palace where they would meet the most exalted company of the day.

The gossip barely ceased from New Year's Day to Carnival Sunday as society danced and chatted and went to theatres, concerts and ballet, and chatted and danced and chatted yet again. The grey-flanked, snow-covered streets of St Petersburg were bright with *troikas* driven by coachmen in scarlet-caped coats and brightly-coloured three-cornered caps, trimmed with gold braid and fur. The British Embassy staff patriotically wore a red, white and blue cockade in their caps.

It was the Dowager Empress who chaperoned her two eldest grandchildren to a small dance Marie Pavlovna gave early in the winter of 1913. The young girls – fair-haired, blue-eyed Olga, aged eighteen, and Tatiana, slender, with dark hair and light brown eyes, and a year younger – were already very attractive young women. They danced every dance and were quite evidently enjoying themselves. Their grandmother, resplendent in white and ablaze with diamonds, watched the scene with her quick, bright, dark eyes which saw everything even when she was engaged in conversation with her neighbour. She was known for her great charm and for the indulgence she showed to her Court. She never forgot a face or missed a point or failed to say exactly the right thing to the right person. Her small figure, often clad in black, was a frequent sight in St Petersburg, driving in an open carriage or sleigh with an enormous black-bearded Cossack standing on the running board behind her.

The social event of the season was in fact a ball that the Dowager Empress herself gave for her granddaughters at her own Anitchkov Palace, erected on the Nevsky Prospect in the eighteenth century by the Empress Elizabeth from the designs of Rastrelli. Alexandra did appear on this occasion, but she left early, and it was the Tsar who remained until 4.30 in the morning to take his daughters home to Tsarskoe Selo.

The Anitchkov Palace was also the setting for the wedding on 22 February 1914 of Prince Felix Youssoupov to Princess Irina, daughter of the Grand Duke Alexander and the Tsar's eldest sister, Grand Duchess Xenia. Irina, quite beautiful at any time, was exquisite in her wedding dress of white satin embroidered

Prince Felix
Youssoupov and his
beautiful wife
Princess Irina, the
Tsar's niece.

in silver, with its long train. Her lace veil, which had belonged
to Marie Antoinette, was gathered into a tiara of rock crystal
and diamonds. She drove up in a coach drawn by four white
horses and entered the chapel on the arm of the Tsar to take
her place beside her bridegroom, who was wearing the uniform
of the nobility: a black frock-coat with collar and lapels embroidered in gold, and white broadcloth trousers. The young
couple were overwhelmed with gifts, including the most gorgeous jewels. The Tsar offered Felix an office at the Court as his
contribution, but Felix preferred to choose the privilege of using
the imperial box at the theatre.

Felix's parents gave them the ground floor of the left wing of their house on the Moika in which to start their married life. Entered by a short flight of white marble steps lined with statues, it contained a ballroom with yellow marble columns ending in great arcades which opened on to a winter garden. Next to this was the large drawing-room hung with ivory silk and decorated with paintings of the eighteenth-century French school. The French restoration furniture was gold and white wood covered with ivory silk embroidered with flowers. Felix's own private sitting-room was even more striking – the mahogany furniture was covered in bright green material with an embroidered centre design, and the sapphire-blue walls were adorned with Gobelin tapestries and Dutch paintings. The hangings in the library were also emerald-green, this time superbly set off by Karelian birch-wood panelling. The main colour of the dining-room was amethyst, a fitting background to the great illuminated glass-fronted cabinets filled with the family collection of Archangel-skoie porcelain from their own factory. The ceilings were painted grey and decorated with stucco work throughout, while Aubusson carpets, rock crystal chandeliers and a general abundance of *objets d'art* were standard features. Facing the courtyard, the young couple had their own small chapel and private apartments, and in this vicinity there was also a mosaic swimming pool. To the left of the entrance, Felix had his own *pied-à-terre*, which was later to assume international significance as the scene of a momentous murder.

Also that winter one of the most famous hostesses of the day, Countess Marie Kleinmichel, gave in her house on Sergeevskii Street one of her fancy-dress balls which provided food for discussion for the remainder of the season. No malicious criticism clouded her reputation. She was a *grande dame* down to her aristocratic finger-tips, and there was no one who did not deem it an honour to accept her invitations. She rarely left the house as she was something of a cripple, but despite this she had an uncanny knack of learning the intimate secrets of practically everyone in society, and her home was a veritable hotbed of gossip. Rich and eccentric, she, in common with many other members of St Petersburg society, dabbled in the occult. Princess Obolensky once took her sceptical husband to a seance at this house. At the height of the proceedings, when all the lights were out, a piercing scream was emitted by Countess Kleinmichel. 'Shall I put on the lights?' asked Prince Obolensky innocently. 'On no account', came the stern reply. When the seance was over and light was finally restored, the fact was revealed that the Countess had her wig on upside-down. 'A naughty ghost must have snatched off her wig', was Prince Obolensky's comment. His wife never took him to a seance again.

Her ball in January 1914 was one of the biggest and most magnificent of the season, though she herself apologetically stated that only 300 invitations were sent out. Her house could not hold more, and as it was the Russian custom to serve dinner at small tables, the kitchen would be taxed to capacity. Several set quadrilles were danced in costumes of different periods, by far the most spectacular being the Persian quadrille led by the Grand Duchess Cyril and the Grand Duke Boris, leaders of the younger 'smart set'. Most of the women and many of the men had costumes specially designed for the evening by the fashionable Jewish artist and theatrical designer Leon Bakst. Bakst was there in person that evening and put the crowning touch to Princess Paley's happiness. 'Your son', he said to her, 'is the Prince Charming who is dreamed of in fairy tales.' The Princess had taken infinite pains over seventeen-year-old Vladimir's costume. Following the fashion of the period of Tsar Alexis Mihailovich, it consisted of a tight-fitting white coat embroidered in gold, loose blue silk trousers, red shagreen boots and a white cloth cap with wide bands of sable. The young diplomat Nicolas de Basily modelled his costume on a portrait of a Venetian dignitary of the Renaissance period and arrived richly dressed in crimson silk.

Countess Betsy Shouvalov gave two big balls that year in the colossal Empire-style ballroom of her palace on the Fontanka Canal which had its own private stage, a magnificent marble staircase and an imposing series of reception rooms. One of these balls was a complete symphony in black and white. The guests at the other one went in splendid wigs or gaily coloured turbans.

There was no end to the balls in that fateful season of 1914, hostesses vying to outdo each other in glamour and originality. Princess Olga Orlov, another outstanding figure of society, and Prince Vladimir Orlov, head of the Tsar's private secretariat, gave a great party in their big white palace on the Moika. Both husband and wife were very popular, and the Countess was reputed to be one of the best-dressed women in the world, with a lovely figure and a distinguished manner. The Prince, des-

cended from a lover of Catherine the Great, was a highly cultivated man with a sarcastic tongue; he was nicknamed 'Fat Orlov' or '*l'homme chien*' because he looked so much like a well-bred dog. He had once been a cavalry officer, but now his rolls of fat made it impossible for him to mount a horse, and he was forced to follow processions on foot.

The Polovzovs gave a party that winter in their Empire-style residence on the Islands. They had earned a reputation for inviting only beautiful women, good dancers and amusing people. As a result, their functions were never overcrowded; the flowers were tasteful but never ostentatiously over-abundant; and Goulesko's gipsy band was always engaged to play. An additional attraction to their entertaining consisted of the two big

Countess Marie Kleinmichel, the famous hostess, and the dashing Prince Felix Youssoupov, both in historical costume for one of the many sumptuous fancy-dress balls held in fashionable St Petersburg.

45

A lavish interior
crowded with gilt,
marble and mirrors,
typical of those in which
the St Petersburg rich
held their social
functions. Thousands
of beautiful women
in satin and jewels
would have floated
elegantly down stairs
like these, the Jordan
Staircase in the
Hermitage.

ice-hills in their grounds – these were wooden structures some fifty to sixty feet high and covered with thick layers of ice. In the afternoon, the guests would sport on these hills, mounting them by steps cut in one side and descending at great speed on a toboggan down the other – the gentlemen sat in front and steered, while the lady knelt behind him with her hands on his shoulders. Tired but exhilarated, the guests would come into the house for tea, change their clothes, and then dance the night away. Outside the windows, flares turned the ice-hills and gardens into a veritable fairyland.

These were just the highlights of that season. There were two dances at the British Embassy and the usual large balls at the German Embassy. Count Berchtold, the Austrian Ambassador, gave a brilliant *cotillon* over Christmas 1913. Enormous quantities of flowers had been imported from the Riviera; each lady had a basket beside her, and every time a man asked a lady to dance, he presented her with a bouquet. Extremely valuable favours were exchanged at this *cotillon* – Serge Obolensky, for example, received a very fine cigarette case. There were several dances for which the ladies chose their own partners and each pinned a medal on the man of her choice. The most popular dancers emerged beribboned and decorated, great heroes of the ballroom.

To enable St Petersburg society to dance for almost every night of the week during the short period between New Year's Day and Lent, there was always a fair assortment of *bals blancs* and *bals roses*. The *bals blancs* were mainly held for young debutantes, and consequently large numbers of young guards officers in their brilliant uniforms were invited. There was rarely an orchestra. Its place was taken by a pianist, a *tappeur*, who accompanied the dancers as they followed the shouted instructions of a red-faced, perspiring master of ceremonies through the numerous quadrilles. Very few waltzes and two-steps were danced on these occasions, though later in the evening the series of dancing-games known as *cotillons* were usually requested. For the young people the *cotillons* were slightly different from the one arranged by the Austrian Ambassador. They all sat around the room on little golden chairs while vast quantities of flowers were brought in: market baskets full of golden daffodils, masses of Parma violets, lilac, bunches of roses, carnations, hyacinths and lilies of the valley. Again, they had all been brought at enormous expense in specially heated carriages from the South of France. Then a high hedge entirely covered with roses would be wheeled in and, standing on tip-toe, the girls would lean over it and touch the hand of an unseen partner on the other side, while yet again the master of ceremonies shouted directions and distributed favours of broad satin ribbons with gold and silver balls and flowers. And all the while the chaperones, uniformly dressed in purple, black and grey satins, with fur stoles round their shoulders, pearls round their necks, and their hair pulled plainly back from their faces, sat on the sidelines, watching attentively the behaviour of their young charges and smiling benignly the while.

The *bals roses*, given by young married women, were much less formal. There were hardly any *cotillons* but as many waltzes as the most enthusiastic young dancer could desire. And to add to the hilarity of the occasion, there was usually a band, Colombo's or Goulesko's gipsy band, for gipsy music was supposed to reach to the depths of the Russian soul. One Russian lady was even reputed to employ gipsies to play in the room next to her boudoir when she received her lover.

But it was at one of the big balls to which everyone (who was anyone, that is) was invited that Meriel Buchanan met and fell in love with Duke Alexander of Leuchtenberg. Who could have resisted his good looks, enhanced by his blue and gold uniform with the gold *aiguillettes* which proclaimed him ADC to the Tsar? It was at the Palace of Madame Serebriakov that they met, but the romance continued in and out the intricacies of the St Petersburg season.

On the few evenings when there was no ball, society people could go to the ballet at the Maryinsky Theatre. It was very difficult to get seats in the white and gold auditorium with its blue curtains and chairs and its deep blue carpet, as nearly all the stalls and boxes were permanently booked, passing on by hereditary right from father to son. The pressure was increased by the fact that no 'lady' could sit anywhere but in a box. It was also considered unseemly for her to remain in it during intervals. Hence, directly the curtain fell, everyone retired to an ante-room behind their boxes to smoke, chat, gossip and receive visits from young men. Writing some twenty years later, Meriel Buchanan still recalled:

. . . the individual atmosphere of that huge theatre, the scent of *ambre* and *chypre*, of chocolates and cigarettes, the faint smell of

49

ABOVE A seat at the
ballet in the Maryinsky
Theatre automatically
implied social position,
sinces boxes and stalls
were 'owned' on a
permanent basis and
passed on from one
generation to the next.

OPPOSITE For those
who preferred more
invigorating outdoor
pastimes in the winter,
bear-hunting on one's
estates was an exciting
prospect.

heating, of leather and of the age-old dust raised by hundreds of
dancing feet. I can visualize the white and blue and gold of the
decorations, the four tiers of boxes, the dim faraway gallery, the
parterre of stalls crowded with artists, musicians, young diplomats,
officers in brilliant uniforms, old bald-headed generals. Now and
then, defying convention, a young girl would lean from a box to
smile a greeting at some young man below; a few old men, grouped
together in earnest discussion, would for once not be talking politics
but would be arguing about the technique of some dancer's step,
shaking their heads mournfully as they agreed that the true art of
choreography was deteriorating, and that the last ballets lacked the
beauty of the older productions. Fat ladies of the merchant classes
munched chocolates brought to them in beribboned boxes by portly
men with smooth faces; outside in the foyer young girls and boys
from the gallery seats would walk solemnly round and round,
watched by some anxious mother, sitting eating cream cakes and
drinking weak sugared tea. . . .

Male members of the social circle had a refuge of their own.
This was the Yacht Club reserved for the élite and frequented
by several Grand Dukes as well as ministers and other influential
personages. Many a career began and ended there; many a repu-

tation was made and unmade; many a fortune was won or lost at the gaming tables. The solidarity that existed between members of the Yacht Club reflected, or was a continuation of, the *esprit de corps* bred at the secondary school most of them had attended. This was the Imperial Alexander *Lycée* founded by Alexander I in 1811 to prepare sons of noblemen for careers in the service of the State. A hundred years later the boys still wore the same uniform; a dark green frock-coat with a row of golden buttons and a red collar with gold braid, and a black three-cornered hat. Senior students also carried swords, which were passed on from class to class. Nicholas II visited the school regularly and informally, and the boys reciprocated with almost unqualified support of the monarchy. They carried this with them in later life together with their loyalty to each other and to their *alma mater*, and renewed their bonds when students past and present gathered there every year on founder's day, 1 November.

On the first day of Lent everything ceased. In the Russian Orthodox Church, Lent begins at midnight on the Sunday before Ash Wednesday. To make the most of that last Sunday, known as '*La Folle Journée*', it was often spent at a country

OVERLEAF The perfect stillness of a Russian winter. A horse-drawn sleigh waits outside a country house.

estate near St Petersburg in general merrymaking. Lunch would be served. The party would drive out through snow-covered woods in open sleighs, stopping only to play games on ice-hills or to indulge in snowball fights. The day would culminate in a dance in the evening – which stopped the moment the clock struck twelve.

Dinner parties now replaced the balls. These began in a separate room where the special Russian *hors d'œuvres, zakhouska*, were set out on long white-covered tables. Washed down with vodka, these *zakhouska* could include stuffed eggs served with a spiced sauce, smoked salmon, button mushrooms in hot cream, caviare, small salted cucumbers, vegetable salad, slices of ham, cold smoked fish, little hot cocktail sausages flavoured with wine. . . . The already well-fed guests would then move on to the dining-room where the formal meal was then served – it could begin with red cabbage soup or beetroot soup (*borscht*) served with soured cream and hot pastries. This would be followed by sturgeon or sterlet, roast venison and a form of partridge which tasted rather like grouse. Then came the dessert – perhaps a blend of fruit and cream and nuts. In between courses, footmen would bring round jewelled boxes of little yellow cigarettes. Then the company would adjourn to play bridge, to listen to music, or to talk politics or fashion.

The round of gaiety resumed in the summer – only its location changed, as everyone departed for their estates and St Petersburg was almost deserted. Tsarskoe Selo was a particular centre of attraction. A wide tree-shaded boulevard running from the railway station to the park around the imperial family's Summer Palace was lined with the houses of the nobility, standing in their own grounds. Many of society's leaders had villas there and entertained lavishly. Grand Duke Boris had an English-style country house built by Maples and equipped with an English butler and coachman. The Youssoupovs had a pavilion which Felix's grandmother had had copied from a house that Nicholas I had offered to give her as a present. It was a Louis xv-style residence, painted entirely white both inside and out. In the centre of the building was a large room with six doors leading to the drawing-rooms, dining-room and garden. The furniture, of the same period as the house, was also painted white and was covered with flowered cretonne. Long cretonne curtains lined with buttercup yellow silk hung at the windows.

Officers stationed at the near-by military camp at Krasnoe

Selo came over to Tsarskoe to join dinner parties or bridge parties or dances. Special trains brought guests unavoidably detained in the quiet city down for special events, such as enormous picnics held in the woods under coloured awnings where luncheon consisting of the choicest delicacies would be served by footmen in livery. Nathalie Majolier supplies a typical menu for such a picnic: beginning with caviare and smoked salmon, it would proceed through cold game to cold sturgeon with vegetable salad and horseradish sauce. If the day were not too hot, a fire would be built and sausages and potatoes baked in the embers. Later, they would lounge under the trees playing bridge, dance on specially constructed wooden platforms, bathe or go boating on the lakes until it was time for fleets of limousines to carry them, exhausted, back to the train.

Special trains, and private coaches which could be hooked on to ordinary trains, both had their part to play in Russian social life. The Youssoupov family certainly had one to carry them around to their numerous estates, stretching over the length and breadth of Russia, and on the whole they found it considerably more comfortable than many of the disused manor houses they stayed in on arrival. The coach was entered by a vestibule, which in the summer became a veranda containing an aviary. Dining- and drawing-room were combined in one mahogany-panelled compartment where the chairs were upholstered in green leather and the windows hung with yellow silk. The bedrooms of the various members of the family were panelled in light wood and hung with bright chintzes. Other apartments were reserved for friends and for the large staff of servants who accompanied the Youssoupovs on their trips. There were, of course, also a private kitchen and bathroom. A similarly equipped coach stood permanently idle at the Russo–German frontier in case it was required for trips abroad.

Even the British Ambassador had a special carriage reserved for him when he arrived in Russia in 1910. The comfort and luxury of the sitting-room upholstered in blue brocade struck him forcibly. The American Ambassador, George Marye, was equally favourably impressed by the special train provided to take members of the Diplomatic Corps to Tsarskoe Selo to offer their New Year congratulations to the Tsar on New Year's Day 1915. Here again, it was the sitting-room that caused most surprise, with its roomy easy chairs. And this was for a journey that took only half an hour. Nor did the sense of opulence

One of the Tsar's private trains in the little station at Tsarskoe Selo.

diminish when he left his carriage. A Court equipage with a coachman and footmen in the brilliant livery of the imperial household drove him the half mile to the palace.

The Tsar's private train was equipped on an even more lavish scale. In fact, the Tsar had two identical trains, for security reasons. Both were painted blue with coats-of-arms and monograms, and both consisted of eight coaches. Both left on the day the Tsar intended to make a journey, but nobody knew (except, that is, for the organizers) which carried the imperial household. The most impressive feature of the train was the drawing-room in the third coach; panelled in mahogany, it was heavily curtained, and the furniture was upholstered in damask velvet. It even contained a piano. The royal couple's private apartments occupied the whole of the fourth coach. They included a fully equipped private bathroom as well as the Tsar's study, complete with desk, armchairs in his favourite green leather and a bookcase, and the Tsarina's sitting-room, upholstered in grey and lilac. The fifth coach was the nursery, a dream of bright cretonne and white furniture.

Very often it was to Livadia, the imperial family's favourite home in the Crimea, that this train travelled. The Crimea was also a popular holiday resort for the aristocracy, many of whom had estates along the south coast between the ports of Sebastopol and Yalta. The Youssoupovs in fact had several estates there, but visited only two of them: Koreiz on the Black Sea, and Kokoz in the heart of a valley surrounded by high mountains. The luggage the family took with them on these occasions was very considerable, and the number of servants equally so. They were nothing, however, Prince Felix tells us, in comparison with the entourage that accompanied Count Alexander Sheremetev. He took not only his servants and their families but also his musicians and a few cows so that the children could have fresh milk on the journey. At Koreiz the Youssoupovs stayed in a rather ugly grey stone house set in a park, with gardens and vineyards stretching terrace upon terrace down to the seashore. The air was redolent with the perfume of thousands of La France roses. Pavilions to accommodate guests were erected in the park, which was crammed with statuary – naiads and goddesses

The warm and sultry south. The terrace of a hotel at Yalta in the Crimea, a fashionable holiday resort among the aristocracy.

57

peeped out of every bush and thicket. On the seashore, Prince
Felix's father had built a pavilion and a swimming pool where
the water was kept at a pleasant temperature all the year round.

At Kokoz, near a small Tartar village, Felix's mother had
built a house in the local style. It was large and white and beautiful, reminiscent of the Khan's palace at Bakhtchisarai. Outside,
the roof was covered with old glazed tiles which had mellowed
to soft shades of green. Inside, the furniture was copied from
old Tartar pieces and painted red, blue and bright green, while

oriental fabrics covered the divans and walls. The dining-room had Persian stained-glass windows and a marble fountain copied from one in the Khan's palace. To tone in with their surroundings, guests were encouraged to don oriental robes (a selection was kept available) before appearing for dinner. Western-type entertainments were also provided, however. Guests could, if they so wished, fish for trout from a balcony in the small stream that ran by the gate.

Felix's mother had another stake in the Crimea. Her husband had, as a birthday present one year, given her a completely bare mountain, Ai-Petri, towering over the south coast.

The society the Youssoupovs enjoyed included Countess Kleinmichel whose Crimean home was noted for its library of books on Freemasonry. Countess Panine also lived near by in a kind of castle, where she entertained politicians, artists and writers, including Leo Tolstoy and Anton Chekov. Grand Duke Alexander Mikhailovich's estate, Ai-Todor, was also in the vicinity – a beautiful old house, its walls covered in roses and wistaria. Also wistaria-covered was Aloupka, the Voronstovs' home near Sebastopol, with a park decorated with fountains and statues. All these estates were near Yalta, the centre for excursions and the home port of the imperial yacht *Standart*.

Another holiday centre of the aristocracy was in the Baltic provinces. Those members of the nobility who had houses there, such as the Grand Duke Cyril, organized an automobile club among themselves, and held an annual motor rally which they called the *Victoria-Fahrt* in honour of Cyril's wife, Grand Duchess Victoria. Known as 'Ducky', this Grand Duchess was a grand-daughter of Queen Victoria.

In the middle of June 1914, a wave of excitement broke St Petersburg's summer quiet. The first British battle-cruiser squadron, under the command of Sir David Beatty, anchored just outside Kronstadt. British and Russian flags hung from every window. British sailors thronged the streets around the port, and Russian crowds flocked to the quays to gaze curiously at two small cruisers that had come up the Neva and anchored just below the Nicholas Bridge. Every day of the visit was filled with social activity. A dinner was held at the British Embassy, and a dinner and dance at the Town Hall. Beatty and his officers lunched with the Tsar at Tsarskoe Selo and reciprocated by entertaining the whole imperial family to lunch on board the English flagship. Later, there was a ball on the *Lion* and the *New*

The Khan's palace at Bakhtchisarai in the Crimea, on which Felix Youssoupov's mother based the design for her holiday home at Kokoz.

59

The pomp and elegance of a Court function. President Poincaré of France is presented by the Tsar (behind Poincaré) to the Tsarina Alexandra.

Zealand roped together. The Grand Duke Boris gave a party for the visitors in his villa at Tsarskoe Selo.

Barely had the British party sailed off when new guests arrived. In July 1914 President Poincaré of France arrived in St Petersburg. On 20 July he was formally welcomed at a banquet at the Peterhof Palace, an eighteenth-century building kept virtually unchanged since the days of Peter the Great. According to the French Ambassador, Maurice Paléologue,

Thanks to the brilliance of the uniforms, superb toilettes, elaborate liveries, magnificent furnishings and fittings, in short the whole panoply of pomp and power, the spectacle was such as no Court in the world can rival. I shall long remember the dazzling display of jewels on the women's shoulders. It was simply a fantastic shower of diamonds, pearls, rubies, sapphires, emeralds, topaz, beryls – a blaze of fire and flame.

The Tsarina Alexandra added to the brilliance of the occasion in a low brocade gown with a diamond tiara on her head. But, as at many such functions, she was ill at ease and struggling with hysteria.

The following day there was a banquet in honour of the President at the French Embassy. On a carpet of roses and orchids, some ninety-six guests were magnificently served. On 22 July there was a 'Tsaria' or evening review in honour of Poincaré's visit. The Tsar, mounted on a white horse, followed by the Grand Dukes, led a procession of carriages upholstered in white satin bearing the Tsarina, the French President, the Tsarevich and the young Grand Duchesses. The white horses, the outriders in scarlet and gold, the wide flower-trimmed hats and the smiling faces of the young girls created a scene of incomparable beauty. Then the Tsar rode forward alone to receive the day's report from all the commanding officers of the guards regiments who advanced one by one to stand at attention before him, each accompanied by a sergeant carrying the regimental flag. Later that evening there was a banquet and a performance at the wooden summer theatre at which all the best artistes of opera and ballet performed.

Less than a week later, the Tsar was to face his people to tell them that their country was at war.

3 The Dispossessed

In July 1914, while the French President Poincaré was paying his colourful State Visit to Russia, while society danced and chatted in the brilliant round of celebrations held in his honour, while diplomatic circles gravely contemplated the various ultimata that would shortly lead to the Great War, a general strike was declared in St Petersburg. Red flags were flourished. Crowds marched through the streets singing the '*Marseillaise*' and other revolutionary songs. Scuffles of varying degrees of violence broke out between workers and police. Stones were hurled, shots exchanged and barricades erected. A slightly bewildered Monsieur Paléologue, only just arrived in the country, noted: 'When I returned to St Petersburg by rail at a quarter to one in the morning, I heard that this afternoon the principal factories went on strike – for no reason and on a signal from no one knows where. There have been collisions with the police at several points. . . .'

There was, in fact, no mystery about the original cause of the strike. It had begun in Baku where an outbreak of plague in the neighbourhood of the oilfields gave rise to a demand for better housing conditions for oil-workers. A general strike in Baku had ensued, which in turn engendered a one-hour sympathy strike in St Petersburg. To the original demands, the strikers in the capital added the call 'For the eight-hour day! For a democratic republic and the confiscation of private land! For socialism!'

The agitation and demonstrations which followed resulted in violent disturbances at the St Petersburg Putilov works. Two workers there were killed by police, about fifty wounded and over a hundred arrested. As a result, the inflamed strikers decided to extend the strike to three days. 'Let a shout of protest and indignation spread throughout all St Petersburg, all Russia . . . only through our own strength will we throw off the autocrat and his gang of brigands.' Not until the outbreak of the war did the violence cease.

The Russian worker did indeed have much to complain of. The industrial working class in Russia had, as we have noted, been late to form because of the late development of Russian industry. Even in 1914 it was a tiny proportion of the total population. Its evolution had followed different lines from that in other European countries. The principal divergence lay in the close link between industrial and agricultural labour in Russia. To begin with, it was, of course, from the passive peasant popu-

PREVIOUS PAGES
Log cabin houses in the Volga valley.

A peasant leaves his
native village to trudge
to the town in search
of work.

lation that the industrial proletariat had so recently been drawn.
Very rarely did the peasant who left the land to work in a factory
entirely sever his connections with his rural origins. Often he
continued to send a portion of his wages home. If he were sick,
or when he grew old, he would retire to the country. Often he
went home at harvest time to lend a hand. Furthermore, industrial wages were so low, and living conditions so difficult, that
quite frequently the worker could not afford to keep his family
with him in the city. A survey of workers' budgets in 1908–10
showed that only the skilled or semi-skilled, earning a minimum
of 400 roubles a year, could afford this luxury. The family more
often had to remain on the land while the wage-earner lived
apart in the town. Conversely, the peasant often left his farm
at times when there was little work required on the land, to
supplement his meagre income by working in a factory.

Parted from wife and children, the conditions in which the

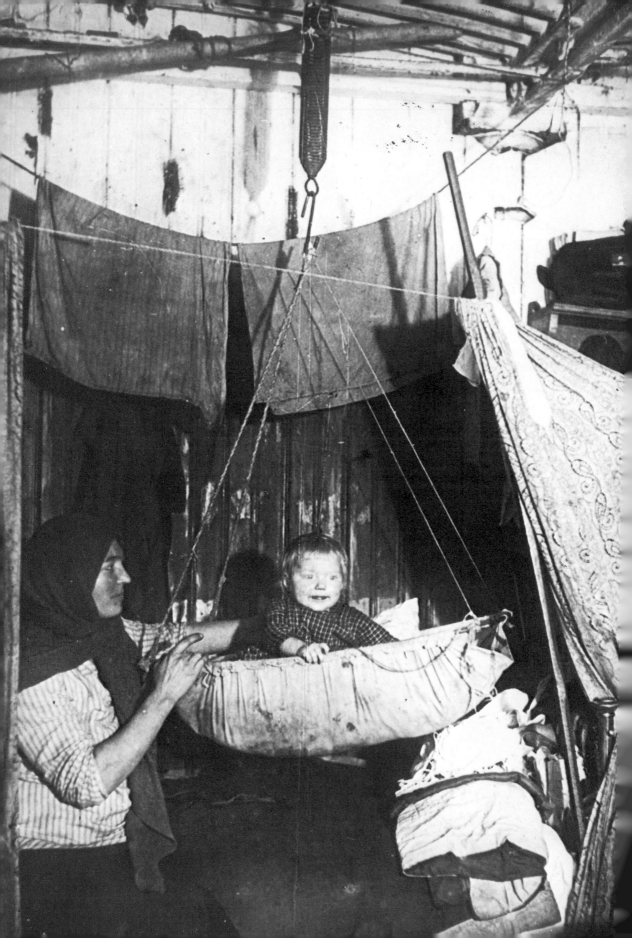

factory worker lived in the early years of the twentieth century left much to be desired. In Baku for example, where the July 1914 strike broke out, almost all the employees lived in barracks built by the oil companies. These buildings had very few windows and were inadequately ventilated. They were heated by oil stoves which, apart from the fire risk they presented, were dirty, smelly and sooty; and all the buildings were crammed to overflowing with beds made solely of planks. Some companies, where work was done in shifts, provided beds for only half the total number of workers, so that bunks were exchanged as shift relieved shift. In other barracks, married couples lived side by side with single men, sometimes separated by a low curtain, sometimes with nothing at all between them. A report in 1903 told how 'the workers, all in greasy, soot-covered rags, covered with a thick layer of grime and dust, swarm like bees in the extremely dirty and congested quarters. A repulsive smell hits you as soon as you try to approach the window.'

In Moscow and St Petersburg conditions were generally no better. The workers were often housed in tenements on the outskirts of the city where land was cheap. Reports of the period abound in lurid details of these dwellings: 'An impossible atmosphere – exhalation of people, wet clothing and dirty linen; everywhere dampness and dirt. Draughts in every corner; in rainy weather water on the floor two inches deep.' '. . . the atmosphere was intolerably stuffy because of the density of the inhabitants. The apartment is damp and unbelievably dirty. In two rooms there is complete darkness. The ceiling is so low that a tall man cannot stand upright. A specific smell.' 'The apartment has a terrible appearance, the plaster is crumbling, there are holes in the walls, stopped up with rags. It is dirty. The stove has collapsed. Legions of cockroaches and bugs. No double window frames, and so it is piercingly cold. The lavatory is so dilapidated that it is dangerous to enter, and children are not allowed in. All the apartments in the house are similar.' Inspectors also noted people of all ages and both sexes sleeping intermingled in this accommodation, with only low curtains separating the beds.

Conditions were even worse in the small factories where work was done by hand or by simple technical means, such as those of the silk, woollen or textile-printing industries. Here it was quite usual for workers and their families to live, eat and sleep on the factory floor. In a workshop specializing in swingling

Squalid living conditions in a workers' hostel in Moscow.

flax and hemp, this could be particularly uninviting. Beneath bundles of dripping discoloured fibres which blocked out any daylight that might otherwise have entered through the grey, smeared windows, surrounded by clumsy machines for breaking up the fibres, the family would squat on a floor covered with a thick layer of sticky, nauseating filth, in between steaming buckets and pools of dark water, to eat their crude meals. At night they would bring planks and lie down to sleep with bundles of fibre as pillows. The floor was scraped clean once a year, but little was done about the cracked, mildewed walls and crumbling plaster. In the heat and damp necessary for processing the fibres, mothers nursed their children, and babies wailed in their cradles.

Sometimes, especially in the big cities, the worker would rent his own apartment and bring his wife and family to live with him there. This 'apartment' would generally consist of one small, dark room, furnished in the most rudimentary fashion, with a bed, two chairs and a table. All the rooms opened on to a common corridor. To make ends meet, the family would often take an unattached worker as a tenant, giving him a bed in a screened-off section of the already tiny room in exchange for rent. He was also given his food, which invariably consisted of black bread, sauerkraut, cabbage soup, boiled buckwheat with bacon, fresh cucumbers in summer, salted cucumbers in winter, and *kvass* – the typical, unchanging peasant diet. The worker who slept and ate at the factory was, from this point of view, slightly better off in that he was actually given meat at lunchtime. In this case, the price of the employee's meals was deducted from his wages. Some factories also maintained shops where the worker could buy on credit – the bills he ran up were again subtracted from his pay.

For lodgings like those described above, the worker would pay something like 3·15 roubles a month in St Petersburg in 1908, out of an average monthly wage of twenty-two roubles. It is little wonder that his expenditure listed under 'recreation and cultural needs' was minimal – one example lists twenty-eight kopecks on bath-houses, eighteen kopecks on postage, fourteen kopecks on tram fares and ten kopecks on theatres and cinemas. It also included the money spent by the worker on drink at the *traktir*, the Russian equivalent of the English public house. Their city homes could hold little attraction for the Russian workers, and they spent much of their time at the *traktir* drinking tea, vodka or beer – with the emphasis mainly on tea.

The large family of a St Petersburg metal worker were only able to rent the corner of this room.

68

The *traktir* differed from the English pub in that the customers sat mainly at tables, and the wooden counter which ran the entire length of one side of the room was used solely for serving and for displaying bottles, glasses, and plates of sausages and ham. There was no lounging at the bar. Instead, a host of waiters in white blouses, white trousers and white aprons ran hither and thither taking customers' orders. Against one wall hung a candle-lantern with the word TRAKTIR painted on it in brown. On another hung an enormous gilt ikon. The heavy door creaked miserably to admit newcomers, its reluctance inviting compari-

Women workers at
a Moscow textile mill
receive their meagre
mid-day meal from the
communal stove.

son with the easy entry swing-doors gave to American bars. Apart from the crowd of working men and women who came there to drink and to talk, a stream of extraneous characters moved in and out of the *traktir*. A blind musician would enter and seat himself at a table to play the melancholy strains of traditional Russian tunes on the concertina or violin. A pedlar would appear moving from group to group offering pies for sale or Bibles, shirts, pencils or old clothes, coping ably with the bargaining and haggling his clientele considered an indispensable feature of a sale. Beggars, cripples and dwarfs would slouch in, asking for alms in the name of Christ. Drunken hooligans would try to cadge free drinks, and pilgrims from faraway places would circulate, collecting money to rebuild some church in their home village. It was not unusual for one of the Moscow peasant millionaires – one of the few men of lowly birth who through exceptional shrewdness and business acumen had managed to amass vast fortunes – to stroll casually into a *traktir* and join the company as if he had never moved away from the *milieu*.

And all the time, in an atmosphere thick with smoke, the talk went on. Public meetings were forbidden in Russia. The infor-

A crowded, smoke-filled *traktir*, one of the few pleasures the urban poor could afford, and the scene of heated political arguments since public meetings were illegal.

mal exchange of views that took place in the *traktir* was a very good equivalent. However, the *traktir* did not always get away scot-free. The *Yama* (the Pit), in Rozhdestvensky Street, the most famous Moscow *traktir*, frequented not only by workers but also by scholars and philosophers, was closed down by the government when it became a breeding-ground for too unconventional views. Nevertheless, the *Yama* proved impervious to repressive measures. It reopened in new premises and became 'The Bay' in the Malo-Golovinskaya by the Candlemas Gate. Here, the English writer Stephen Graham was regaled with high-calibre religious discussion and hot cabbage pies, brought in trayfuls from the kitchen by a diminutive serving boy.

When Paléologue inquired about the strike in July 1914 in St Petersburg, he had been told that it was 'instigated by German agents'. 'From the point of view of the Alliance', Monsieur Paléologue noted, 'the incident gives one food for thought.' In fact, responsibility would seem to lie elsewhere. It was from a section of Russia's own intelligentsia – that other dispossessed class – that the instigators of the strike were drawn. Without the promptings of this intelligentsia it is unlikely that the poverty-stricken, uneducated, frequently illiterate Russian workers would have united in any form of combined action against the employers. The ideologies of the educated élite lay behind the mass action of the workers.

This revolutionary intelligentsia was in a sense remote even from the working classes. In June 1905 Maurice Baring went to a meeting held by the Labour group of the Duma in Terrioki in Finland and was particularly struck by this dichotomy. 'You see', he was told by a participant, 'the real workmen can't come to a meeting like this; it's too expensive.' 'There were not many workmen', Baring comments independently, 'but a number of students and various other members of the intelligentsia – young men with undisciplined hair and young ladies with large *art nouveau* hats and *Reformkleider*.' In fact, the whole expedition smacked more of a holiday outing than of world revolution – right from the start when 'the crowd leaped from the train and immediately unfurled red flags and sang the "*Marseillaise*"', to the closing stages when the 'revolutionaries' repaired to the beaches and lay in the sunshine on the grass, continuing the fiery discussion.

The intelligentsia – particularly students – played an important part in inciting the sometimes apathetic workers to demand better treatment.

The universities were hotbeds of dissidence. The sprigs of the nobility who were sent to the Alexander *Lycée* were brought up loyal to the traditions of the autocracy and of state service. Those who went to the big universities at St Petersburg or Moscow or Kiev came into contact with a much wider range of ideas from young men and women drawn from all strata of society, some of whom had to work to support themselves. The young women in floppy hats and the hairy youths whom Baring met in Finland were by no means typical of the *genre*. More frequently seen were the archetypes described by Maurice Paléologue.

Russian students are usually a sorry spectacle, with their haggard faces, drawn features, hollow cheeks, frail figures, thin arms and pronounced stoop. These emaciated bodies in worn-out and tattered clothing are a living witness of the wretched condition of the university proletariat in Russia. Many students have no more than ... one-third of the bare minimum required to support a normal existence in this bleak climate. The result of this defective physiological replacement is not merely a debilitated organism; combined with the strain of an active brain and mental anxieties, it involves the nervous system in a condition of permanent irritation. Hence these melancholy, or fevered, anxious and haggard faces, these fanatical or prematurely aged looks, these features of ascetics, visionaries and anarchists. . . .

The women students [Paléologue continues], of whom there is a large number, repay observation no less. I happened to notice one coming out of a café in the company of four young men: they stopped on the pavement to resume the argument. The tall, pretty girl with bright, hard eyes under her astrakhan cap was laying down the law. Two more students soon came out of the *traktir* and joined the group around her. Here before my eyes I had perhaps one of the most original types of Russian womanhood: missionary of the revolutionary gospel.

The long row of red-fronted buildings on the Vasili Ostrov which housed the University of St Petersburg, founded by Alexander I in 1819, was a particular hearth of student unrest. None of its four faculties was as vociferous as the School of Jurisprudence – which, in any case, took the major portion of the total registration of 7,500 students. Count Benckendorff explains that law was 'the accepted course for all not intending to specialize in any particular way'. Prince Obolensky (himself a law student) suggests that if they had been reading technology, the same problems would not have arisen, and Russia might even have benefited. They would have had no difficulty in finding employment on graduation and would have been able to make a positive contribution to Russia's economic development. As it was, the students had a hearty contempt for physical exercise; they were not allowed to form clubs; and they therefore turned to politics. Numerous debating societies flourished clandestinely, and the university and the system generally bred socialists and revolutionaries by the hundreds. It is an interesting fact that most of the disturbances that shook the nation occurred in term-time, which lasted from 1 September until Easter.

Student revolt was even then no novelty, but the gulf between the Russian student and the establishment in the first decades of the twentieth century was wider than in most other countries. Between 1905 and 1908, for example, 22·9 per cent of those tried for political crimes were members of the liberal professions or students; of these, 9·1 per cent were members of the aristocracy. A survey of a representative selection of students made in 1910 confirms the direction of their political allegiance: twenty-five per cent were affiliated to the Social Democrats; twenty-one per cent to the Kadets; twenty-one per cent were non-party; twelve per cent belonged to the Socialist Revolutionaries; ten per cent were left wing; three per cent belonged to the anarchists, and two per cent to the Octobrists and moderate right.

The Bolshevik Party, the smaller breakaway group of the Social Democrats, had for many years before 1914 been inciting the workers to strike, to overthrow the government, to bring about the revolution. Under the guidance of Vladimir Ilich Lenin, who in 1914 was in exile in Switzerland, agitators went from factory to factory, preaching the doctrine of revolt. They believed that the revolution which would eventually lead to the overthrow of the capitalist system and the establishment of a communist state must originate from the workers. It was therefore among the workers that they continually employed their energies stirring up the spirit of revolt. The success they achieved can be measured in the numbers of strikes recorded in the first two decades of the century.

Every day we must hear [ran one of their publications], now here, now there, that a man has died, and our bloodsuckers continue to stuff their pockets, giving *no* consideration to the men who have died, whose families have lost their breadwinner and are perhaps *dying of starvation*. The whole day we work, pouring out our blood and sweat. Every minute we expose our life to danger, we have no chance to use an essential break, and when there are accidents they accuse us of carelessness! The greed of the capitalists, the long working day, the meagre wage – there is the cause of all accidents. Even the holidays which we have had until now have seemed too much to these beasts of prey, and they have persuaded the government, which is always on the side of the capitalists, to reduce the number of holidays in the year. . . . Comrades, they have fooled us, they have fed long enough on our blood and sweat. . . .

So ran a leaflet put out as early as 1898 by the Ekaterinoslav Union of Struggle for the Emancipation of the Working Class as a protest against accidents at the Bryansk factory. By 1914, though many of the revolutionaries were in exile like Trotsky and Lenin, the techniques of the underground groups which continued to exist in Russia had been brought to a much higher degree of efficiency. They had also achieved a certain aura of respectability with the election of five Social Democrat members to the Duma in 1912.

Lenin returned secretly from exile in 1917, but his influence on the revolutionary movement had been felt both in Russia and abroad for many years.

The Social Democrats believed that the revolution must come from the working classes. The Social Revolutionary Party, on the other hand, assumed that it would come from the largest sector of the population – the peasantry. They were equally active in sending workers to stir up discontent among the rural population and so incite the peasants to revolt. They were, in fact, largely responsible for the continual disturbances in the countryside in the first decade of the twentieth century. That their efforts produced little result in the years immediately preceding the Great War was due to a general rise in the standard of living of the peasant during that period. This was partially the consequence of a series of good harvests but also because of the Stolypin land reforms, in conjunction with a rise in world prices of agricultural products over the period.

Nonetheless, the Russian peasant still had cause for discontent – though his happy-go-lucky fatalism made him, in any case, hard to arouse. By the decree of emancipation issued by Alexander II in 1861, he had become a free man. He was no longer a serf, the exclusive property of his noble master, unable to move without his permission, liable to be bought and sold at will. The Stolypin reforms of 1906–11 had improved his position still further. He was now able to purchase his own land,

Peasants, wearing the
traditional plaited *lapti*
on their feet, take a rest
during haymaking in
Yaroslavl province.

consolidate it into fields, and so use more economic methods of
production if he could afford them. Unfortunately, only a
relatively small proportion of the peasantry could afford them –
or in fact could afford to take advantage of the land consolida-
tion scheme. The poorer peasant had a hard struggle to make
ends meet, and it was customary for him to look around for
other means of supplementing his income from the land. It was
quite common for whole families to engage in home crafts in the
evenings or during the seasons when agricultural work was
undemanding. All in all, it is estimated that some seven or eight
million peasants in Russia were occupied making wooden bowls
or wooden cutlery or leather goods or toys or lace – or a hundred
and one other things, depending on the speciality of the region
in which they lived. A local merchant would often lend the
peasants money to finance these operations or even supply the
raw materials required, in return for the promise of their output,
while a host of agents toured the countryside buying up production at wholesale prices. Sometimes particularly skilled peasants
would organize themselves into teams of craftsmen and offer

their services in the neighbourhood as a means of earning a part-time income.

This contributed to the self-sufficiency that the Russian village almost attained. When Count Benckendorff's mother refurnished her country house, she ordered the team of local peasant carpenters to reproduce copies of her eighteenth-century chairs. When the Count himself rebuilt his farm buildings, he too employed teams of local workers. What is more, all the materials used, except the sheet iron for the roof, were produced on the estate. The bricks were made from his own clay, fired by his own brushwood. The timber was grown and seasoned in his forests, cut by his men, and transported by his horses. On a smaller scale, the peasant household could almost provide for its own needs from items it either grew or produced itself. It even had access to the raw materials for clothing from the live-stock it reared and the hemp and flax it cultivated. Only salt, frozen fish, tea and sugar had to be brought in from outside.

Peasants would leave their homes entirely when winter came, making their presence on the land unnecessary, yielding also to the strong nomadic streak in their nature which had always tempted them to get up and move on. Some went to the nearest city and applied for a police permit to become sleigh-drivers for the few months. Others tried their hand at a little gentle trading, buying shoddy goods at one point and hawking them from village to village. Still others found work elsewhere, at the docks, in road building, in factories.

When spring arrived, they would trickle back to the village. They were all surprisingly alike, these villages, with their small churches, their communal well, and a motley collection of farm-yard animals scratching in the badly-made, dusty roads. There were, in fact, two churches on the Benckendorffs' estate of Kendorskaya, both built of timber. The older one, dating from the second half of the eighteenth century, was very small, and painted a mellow, dark red with a green roof and cupola. It stood in a beautiful setting, surrounded by its old cemetery and within a grove of birches and willows, by a river. The new church, completed some hundred years later, was a symphony of brilliant pinks and greys, with a magnificent golden cupola.

Most villages also had their own mill, and the miller played a major role in village life. He did not limit his activities to grinding corn but also husked oats, buckwheat and millet, stamped felt for boots and sometimes even manufactured cloth.

In payment for his services, he received a part share in the produce and therefore accumulated a stock of most of the local marketable surpluses. Because of this, he often became a sort of amateur village banker. He also tended to fall into the role of village healer, specializing in fallen maidens. His powers in this respect possibly originated in the belief that mill ponds harboured water-maidens and other sprites.

Within the village the poorer peasants generally lived in cabins made of logs stacked closely together and draught-proofed with oakum packing. Inside there was usually only one small room in which the whole family lived, ate and slept. It contained a large stove, blackened with smoke, a rough table, and benches around the walls. In one corner, lit by night-lights, were the ikons to which the visitor had to bow on entering, even before he greeted his hosts, while on a shelf nearby lay a dusty, mildewed, much-thumbed Bible, testimony to the deep religiosity of the Russian peasant. A few earthenware pots and plates, some wooden spoons and goatskins hanging from nails completed the furnishings of this humble abode. Flies flourished in the warm, menagerie-like odour of overcrowded humanity, and swarmed around the copper samovar.

The peasant's daily routine was varied by occasional visits to the bath-house, without which no village was complete. Within its thickly steamy atmosphere, men and women sweated in intense heat, flogged themselves with birch twigs to stimulate circulation and scratched and scoured themselves in a frenzied effort to achieve cleanliness. Afterwards, they would emerge and roll in the snow in winter, or quench their thirst in a *traktir* in summer.

Another welcome interruption to the dull monotony of rural life was the regular visit of the pedlar, who would arrive from unknown far-off regions with an enormous black bundle strapped to his shoulders – and disappear again, with a lighter load, equally into the unknown. Invariably dressed in black – black, old-fashioned frock coat, black waistcoat, with metal or glass buttons, black trousers and black peaked cap – he was always greeted by a delighted crowd which would gather to inspect his wares.

The larger village, like the one on Count Benckendorff's estate at Sosnofka, had a weekly market-day – every Wednesday; the rows of open sheds with counters and shelves which spread out from the *traktir*, forming two or three streets of

A village market in 1910.

shops, were occupied by itinerant traders: drapers, clothiers, bootmakers and cobblers, saddlers and the like. Behind these stalls were parked a motley collection of vehicles and horses which would carry the traders away late on the Wednesday evening, with their unsold stock, to the next market in the vicinity. Where the sheds ceased, they were replaced by lines of rails and posts to which horses and livestock were tethered while they awaited a buyer. Close by were stocks of carts and sledges, agricultural implements and household goods, while in another part of the market the peasant could buy prefabricated timber houses which he would load on to his sledge or

cart and take away with him. The *traktir* often stayed open all night on market-days, filled with buyers and sellers haggling over transactions or celebrating successful deals with vodka.

The general fair which took place for two days over St Sophia's Day in mid-September was just an amplified version of the weekly market, but permeated with a 'harvest festival' spirit of gaiety and well-being. The three-day horse-fair over St George's Day in April was something quite different. Sosnofka lay in the centre of the excellent horse-breeding territory that covered the southern sector of the Tambov province and the whole of Voronesh. Count Benckendorff describes the scene on the eve of St George's Day:

The vast expanse of the market-place would already be filling up with carts, each with a string of horses attached, and nearly all the houses in the village would be full of their quota of guests, mostly customers preparing for the fray. After a few feeble skirmishes on the preceding afternoon, at dawn on St George's Day the serious action started: a subdued roar of combined cries, horses whinnying and stamping, and snatches of song, would be heard even from a distance, and then suddenly you were in the midst of a seething mass of horses, carts and men. Everybody would be shouting at the top of their voice, horses neighing and rearing, especially when a ring for inspection was formed around them; everywhere people could be seen clambering under and over the horses, inspecting their teeth and feeling their fetlocks. Suddenly a lane in the crowd would open, along which, not without danger to the bystanders, one or more carts would proceed at a full gallop; a method of testing cart-horses. . . . In and out of all this commotion the tribes of gipsies would slip, giving advice, buying and selling by proxy and not infrequently chased and beaten up by their infuriated clients. . . .

With the inevitable April showers as often as not the ground would be ankle-deep in mud, in which man and beast had perforce to wallow. . . .

. . . at the same time a restricted part of the square was reserved for transactions of a different and far superior kind. Here were assembled thoroughbreds and half-bred trotters and carriage-horses, whether singly or already assorted in pairs, and *troikas*, artillery- and train-horses and heavy cart-horses for town use. This business was conducted in a more orderly fashion. A number of the crowd wore smart horsey clothes, and quite a few cavalry men and gunners, officers and men, could be seen in uniform, representing remount commissions. Only in one respect were both sections alike; the gipsies were everywhere in both.

Old men play cards on the pavement in the town of Nizhny Novgorod.

But the major events in the peasant's year were the festivals, which occurred with remarkable frequency. These were occasions for great family get-togethers, even the poorest peasant saving up enough money to spend the whole day in feasting. For the young, eating and drinking were only part of the celebrations. They would take themselves off to the meadows where accordions and balalaikas accompanied dancing, singing and general merrymaking. Swings were a common feature of such entertainments: the peasant girls sat astride a plank that was suspended on ropes, while young men stood at either end, maintaining a swaying motion by flexing their knees.

They dressed very carefully for these events, the girls wearing brightly coloured pinafore-dresses over embroidered blouses, with long necklaces of beads jangling as they danced. On their heads some wore the traditional *kokochnik*, a red or blue diadem; others were content to tie a simple scarf over their hair. All the men wore the typical peasant blouse, a long cotton shirt, buttoned down the side, which hung over the cotton or woollen trousers stuffed into their boots. Boots were a sign of elegance amongst the peasantry. Only the very poorest wore *lapti*, sandals made of the plaited bark of the lime tree.

But these celebrations were not the beginning and end of peasant social life. Count Benckendorff remembers as a youth clandestinely attending peasant parties on winter evenings in the company of young peasant girls who worked in the gardens of his estate. For a tiny fee he spent delightful hours drinking tea, singing, and indulging in flirtatious conversations which could end with more clandestine and passionate encounters in the bushes after midnight.

Cutting the village lime trees was also an event, though of a minor nature, carried out in June. It was followed by the delicate operation of detaching the first two layers of bark. The first layer was used for roofing houses; the second was soaked through the summer, dried through the winter, cut into strips and plaited to make *lapti*. Haymaking was another high point in the peasant's year. Maurice Baring, who participated one August, waxed lyrical:

It was a beautiful sight to see the mowing in the sunset by the river: the meadows were of an intense soft green; the sky all fleecy and golden to the west, and black with a great thundercloud over the woods to the east, lit up with intermittent summer lightning.

The mowers were all in different coloured shirts – scarlet, blue, white and green. They mowed till the twilight fell and the thunder-cloud got near to us. . . .

The local peasant population was sometimes enlarged during harvest time by the influx of seasonal labour, employed from St George's Day in April until the Feast of the Virgin Mary in October. The transients were housed by the landowners in barracks and provided not only with a monthly wage but also with home-produced food: flour, meat, fish, vegetables, butter and milk.

Weddings were, of course, events to cap all others. Even in 1914 they were still often arranged with the help of the village matchmaker, who would sip tea with the fathers of the couple concerned and help them to arrange final details. Once his task was completed, the two men would wrap their hands in a coat and strike them together in a token of agreement. In the marriage ceremony itself the young couple, each clutching a lighted candle, faced the village priest, while pages took turns in holding crowns above their heads. The bearded priest gave each a wedding ring and instructed them to kiss, to drink wine from the same goblet and to follow him round the altar three times with their hands tied together. The church was filled with the scent of burning incense, with the singing of the peasant choir and with general good will. The secular celebration which followed, needless to say, consisted largely of feasting.

A host of superstition surrounded the wedding ceremony – and, in fact, most aspects of peasant life. The Russian peasant was by nature intensely superstitious and would watch with interest to see which of the happy pair would first set foot on the carpet in front of the altar, for that one would be the dominant member of the partnership. Likewise, a watchful eye was kept on the candles they clasped, for these would indicate which would survive the other.

4
A Merchant City, Moscow

An old Russian saying has it that St Petersburg was the head of the Russian Empire, Moscow its stomach. St Petersburg was the modern, western-facing capital; Moscow, with its onion-shaped domes, the ancient oriental capital. St Petersburg was the seat of government and administration; Moscow the home of industry and trade. The contrasts between the two cities can be prolonged indefinitely: St Petersburg was the centre of the revised Russian Orthodox religion, Moscow the stronghold of the 'Old Believers', those who had seceded from the official Russian Church in the seventeenth century when the Patriarch Nikon had introduced reforms into Church practice – and whose descendants still adhered to this denial. St Petersburg was dominated by civil servants and nobility; Moscow by its merchants.

In the eighteenth century, when Peter the Great had founded St Petersburg and attempted to move there not only the government but the whole noble class, lock, stock and barrel, he had aimed to make his new city the capital of Russia in every sense. It was a deliberate effort to break away from Moscow, with its strongly Eastern elements and its tradition of mysticism, superstition and religion. He had, to a very large extent, succeeded.

With the rapid late industrialization of Russia which took place only towards the end of the nineteenth century, however, the merchant class, which in the main had never left Moscow, grew strong and flourished. By 1914 the city was the focal point of all the major railway lines of Russia. In fact, many of them converged on one area in the north-east of Moscow, the Red Pond district, which contained three main railway stations as well as much of the trade and industrial concerns. Moscow was the centre of most of the country's big business enterprises and the principal trading-centre of Russia. The real wealth of the nation was certainly accumulated in Moscow in the hands of the large merchants, and as the realization of the importance of economic development to the well-being of the country slowly dawned, so the status of the industrialist and of the merchant city grew. By the war, there was no escaping the fact that adequate supplies of armaments were essential to survival. The leading metallurgist and financier, Alexei Ivanovich Putilov, a multi-millionaire, moved to the forefront of political life. His steel-grey eyes watched over many a high-level conference table and distinguished dinner party. He was consulted by ministers and politicians alike, and he was praised for possessing the

PREVIOUS PAGES
Barbaric, eastern-influenced Moscow presented a very different spectacle from sophisticated, westernized St Petersburg.

86

dominating characteristics of the American businessman – creative instincts, a spirit of initiative, craving for vast undertakings, and a strict sense of reality and the feasible values and forces. Putilov was based in St Petersburg, where the great family business had been established in 1873. He came from a well-to-do family, had attended the University of St Petersburg and had entered the State Service in 1889. By 1914 he was chairman of the Russo–Asiatic bank as well as a director of several financial and industrial enterprises.

Putilov was a typical representative of the new type of Russian businessman. Moscow, however, retained its position as the main centre of business life. Nicholas II himself always recognized the importance of the old capital and never failed to pay his respects to the city and to its prominent citizens. It was also felt to be incumbent on a newly-appointed Chairman of the Council of Ministers, who had in addition retained the post of Minister of Finance, to make his bow to the 'white-walled city'. Count Kokovstov, who found himself in this position in 1912, had to apologize for his delay in putting in an appearance there which, he was told, had offended the merchants. However,

The splendour of the ancient capital. The Krasnaia Ploshchad, now Red Square, with the exotic onion domes of St Basil's Cathedral.

he enjoyed a friendly reception when he finally appeared at the Stock Exchange Club, but the dinner that the prominent manufacturer Grigori Alexandrovich Krestovnikov, chairman of the Moscow Chamber of Commerce, gave in his honour was the scene of a critical attack on government policy. This came from Pavel Pavlovich Riabushinsky, one of the richest millionaires in Moscow, head of a large business and a great patron of the arts. Bernard Pares, attempting to organize an Anglo–Russian exhibition on behalf of the Anglo–Russian Committee in 1913, found Riabushinsky – and another merchant, Alexander Konovalov – most helpful and co-operative. During the war Riabushinsky, too, moved to political prominence as a member of the Moscow Munitions Committee, while Konovalov's home became a meeting-place for leading liberals.

There were indeed fabulous fortunes in the hands of some of these merchants, who yet formed a class apart from the high society of the nobility. In fact, there was no noble high society in Moscow, and the merchants tended not to live a social life as such. As the daughter of the great nineteenth-century merchant Pavel Tretiakov wrote, 'In Moscow everybody lived somehow separately, in a family circle. Each family had its own absorbing inner life, and there simply was no time for social calls.' Moreover, although by the first quarter of the twentieth century many of the most prominent merchants were equal to many of the leading nobles in education, refinement and culture as well as wealth, they showed no desire whatsoever to acquire noble titles, to enter the noble class or even to own land. Tretiakov's daughter records that her father consistently refused to buy land, on the grounds that it should be held only by people who intended to farm it.

In fact, relationships between nobles and merchants were strange if not strained. On the one hand, the merchant wanted to win the goodwill of the aristocracy. One of the largest textile traders, a man called Khludov, lent several hundred thousand roubles to the Grand Duke Nicholas Nicholaevich with no expectation whatsoever of being repaid. He also presented the Dowager Empress with a very fine young Danish hound – which incidentally involved her in a certain amount of embarrassment when it fell foul of her own entourage of little dogs. On the other hand, an element of inverted snobbery also entered the relationship. The playwright and producer Vladimir Ivanovich Nemirovich-Danchenko recalled a conversation with a merchant

OPPOSITE ABOVE Railways played an enormous part in opening up Russia to trade and foreign influence in both the east and west. A rapid building programme was begun in the late nineteenth century, and all the major routes led to Moscow, the business centre of the vast country.

OPPOSITE BELOW The cannon shop in the famous Putilov factory, a photograph taken during the war in 1916. The owner was involved in many other large enterprises and his wealth and power enabled him to exert political influence too.

ABOVE Count Kokovstov, President of the Council of Ministers.

– a very elegant fellow who bought his clothes in London where he had his own tailor. He used to say of a certain noble, 'Why, he's by far too proud – of course, he'll ask me to a ball in his home, or to a rout – but what's that? No, you let *me* invite you, let *me* show you the sort of party I can give. But what's he – with his visiting card!'

The noble, for his part, regarded the merchant with a degree of contempt. A Governor-General of Moscow, Prince Vladimir Dolgoruky, felt duty-bound to invite merchants to official luncheons at his residence. However, his delicate susceptibilities were often offended by the uncouth habits of his guests, and on one occasion he was sorely tempted to remove from his list a particular merchant who committed the grievous sin of drinking red wine with his fish and cutting his asparagus with a knife. Nemirovich-Danchenko, himself of noble birth, quotes a spiteful little poem written by the actor Sadowsky, inspired by the fact that the great textile merchant Savva Morozov had built a magnificent neo-Gothic palace in the fashionable western section of Moscow where once the house of the intellectual Aksakov family had stood:

> This castle wafts a host of thoughts,
> I muse upon the past, reluctantly and sadly:
> Here, where aforetime the Russian mind reigned,
> Now reigns the manufacturer's wit.

This Moscow palace was so talked about that the Grand Duke Serge Alexandrovich expressed a wish to be shown around it. But Morozov was no truckler to the aristocracy. He was pleased to consent – but made sure that he was away from home at the hour fixed and instructed his butler to do the honours.

The male dancer Vaslav Nijinsky showed an intellectual's scorn for the commercial orders when he gave lessons to the children of a millionaire miller, one Sinyagin by name, at 100 roubles an hour.

The family was typical of the Russian merchant class. We were met by our host and hostess, bowing crudely. . . . During the lessons, given in a spacious hall, the whole family and all the servants congregated. Madame Sinyagin, whose face was beautiful, even if she was fat and had short podgy fingers covered with diamonds, the aunts and cousins, the cook, the grooms, the dish-washers, the laundresses and the coachmen – all were there to watch the Sinyagin

hopefuls at their dancing. . . . After the lesson we would be ushered into a huge dining-room and placed in seats of honour where everything expensive was heaped upon us. . . .

The textile millionaire Savva Morozov's neo-Gothic pile in fashionable western Moscow gives some idea of the lifestyle of the merchant class.

Perhaps this segregation of the merchant class, the fact that rarely, as in England, did wealth bring the industrialist into the ranks of the aristocracy, arose from the relatively rigid delineation of classes in Russia. The noble class was clearly marked by status within the bureaucracy. To be a merchant, the Russian had to be enrolled in one of two guilds, paying the requisite fee to the State. The first of these guilds, and the more expensive, comprised the wholesalers; the second, the retailers. Perhaps, on the other hand, the merchant preferred not to align himself with the nobility because he felt far greater affinity with the peasant class. After all, in many cases his own not very distant forebears had themselves been humble peasants. He often still wore the Russian blouse and trousers, even though

his wife ordered her gowns in Paris and embellished them with priceless jewellery.

Batolin, one of the three men who, according to the Grand Duke Alexander, owned Russia on the eve of the First World War (the other two were Yaroshinsky and Putilov), was the son of a serf who had been liberated in 1861. The famous Morozov family was of peasant origin. Morozov's peasant ancestry may have lain behind his concern for the workers he employed. He built light and airy living-quarters for them and their families, improved medical care and reduced the accident rate. His involvement with the lowest stratum of society caused him great mental distress. He came later in life strongly under the spell of Maxim Gorki, the chronicler of the Russian Revolution, spokesman of the working man, and is said to have given large sums of money to revolutionary funds. With his place in the establishment secured by his great wealth based on the expanding industrial production of Russia, and with his sympathies

engaged irrevocably with the unquiet masses, victims of this expansion, the strain became too great. In 1905 he shot himself. Bernard Pares met the then owner of the firm, N. D. Morozov, when he was trying to organize his exhibition in 1913. He described him as one of the younger merchants, very pleasant and by no means illiberal. He was also, in Pares's opinion, entirely typical of the Russian mentality. Morozov kept him talking for one hour, raising every conceivable objection to the exhibition scheme. Finally, when Pares rose to take his leave, the merchant expressed surprise. 'Why are you going?' he asked. 'You've said "no", haven't you?' Pares replied. 'Not quite', answered Morozov.

Many of the rich merchants had even more ignominious ancestry. They were in fact Jews – who had an even more arduous road to travel before they attained affluence. Jews were very much the outcasts of Russian society. Overt and partially concealed anti-Semitism had always been a feature of Russian

A number of Jews used their business acumen to become successful merchants, and were then partially accepted by society, but in general Russia was a land of anti-Semitism. Here Tsarist police pose with the victims of a pogrom.

life. It had confined them to a specific geographical region of the country, the 'Pale of Settlement'. It had circumscribed the professions open to them. It erupted periodically in positive violence when in irrational and totally unpredictable pogroms Jewish communities would be terrorized and devastated (as in Kiev and Kishinev, for example, in 1905, and Bialystok in 1906). It took the form of blood accusations, such as the Beilis case in 1911, when an unsuspecting Jewish workman was accused of the ritual murder of a Christian youth. The trial of Menahem Mendel Beilis in Kiev, which continued through September and October 1913 and which ended in acquittal, aroused public protest throughout the world. In this atmosphere, thousands of Jews had left the country and found asylum in Britain, the United States and elsewhere. Some stayed and plodded wretchedly on in the hostile *milieu*. A few had, by their financial acumen and perspicuity, broken through the stigma that surrounded them and attained social acceptance by their wealth and usefulness. Some Jews reached the very pinnacle of financial eminence. There was, for example, the famous Guenzburg family which came to the fore in the 1840s as a lessee of a liquor monopoly and an army contractor. However, it was the foundation of the Joseph Yevsel Guenzburg bank in St Petersburg in 1859 that really brought the family into prominence. It became one of the chief financial institutions in Russia, contributed significantly to the development of credit financing and was active in raising funds for building railways and developing goldmines.

It was in fact the railway boom of the 1860s that caused the accumulation of some of the greatest fortunes. The Crimean War had proved all too conclusively that Russia was deficient in some of the basic necessities of modern life. The door was wide open for anyone able to take advantage of the opportunities offered. Two Jews were numbered among the four leading railway pioneers: Lazar Solomonovich Poliakov and Ivan Stanislavovich Bliokh. Poliakov, the son of destitute Jews, began life as a small postmaster in southern Russia. By the time of his death in 1888 (he died at the funeral of another Jewish railway magnate, Abraham Moiseivich Warshavsky), he had established a veritable dynasty of financiers and industrialists. Bliokh also had humble Jewish origins and started as a petty railway official in Poland. He used his first earnings to buy himself a course of study at a German university. On his return, he married the daughter of a wealthy banker, changed his religion, widened his banking contracts and then moved into railway building. The other two railway kings had no Jewish obstacles to overcome. Pavel Grigorievich von Derviz had the advantage of a first-class education at the Imperial Law School in St Petersburg. Savva Ivanovich Mamontov came from a family which was already enriched by the liquor trade.

Some part of the immense fortunes that these magnates built up within a relatively short space of time were used on rich living – in 1868 von Derviz retired to the Italian Riviera, where he built himself a palace and lived a life of luxury, leisure and dissipation. Their homes in Moscow and its environs were very grand. They hung the walls with Old Masters. Nemirovich-Danchenko visited a rich merchant, Ushkov, who had a real Rembrandt in his study, and the floor of his reception-room was encrusted with mother-of-pearl. The palace which Savva Morozov built himself has already been mentioned. But these

The drawing-room of a Moscow industrialist, with its piano and birdcage, seems well-furnished and comfortable but lacks the sumptuousness of the St Petersburg palaces. Many merchant families preferred in fact to live less ostentatiously than their wealth would have enabled them to do.

95

men also felt a debt to humanity and a genuine interest in culture. At an individual level, many members of merchant families took music lessons, went regularly to concerts, ballets and theatres, and, what is more, discussed what they had seen with understanding and intelligence afterwards. The conversation at merchant dinner-tables could match anything heard in a noble salon. Their interests, however, as opposed to St Petersburg's worship of all things European, tended to favour Russian intellectual ideas and artists. Moscow put St Petersburg in the shade in its recognition of great native talent. Dargomijsky and

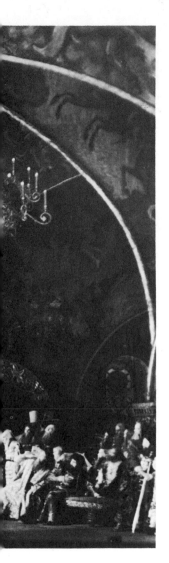

The Boyars' Council meets in the Kremlin, from Act IV of *Boris Godunov*, first brought to Moscow by the merchant and great patron of the arts, Savva Mamontov.

Mussorgsky, Tchaikovsky and Rimsky-Korsakov, Berov, Repin and, of course, Feodor Chaliapin himself, all received their first public acclaim in Moscow.

Poliakov gave a good proportion of his fortune for education and charity. Bliokh wrote a five-volume history of the Russian railways and then devoted his life to working for the cause of world peace. Pavel Riabushinsky published a non-party democratic daily paper, *Utro Rossii*, in Moscow from 1907 until 1917. Savva Mamontov, however, was the greatest philanthropist and art patron of them all. He divided his talents and his interests fairly equally between business and art. A lover of music, he studied in Italy, training his baritone voice, before he used some of his enormous fortune to found the first private commercial opera company in Russia in Moscow in 1885. This gave him the opportunity to put into practice his ideas for employing first-class artists to paint theatrical scenery. It also enabled him to acquaint the Russian public with works by Russian composers which had been coolly received in St Petersburg: Mussorgsky's *Boris Godunov*, Rimsky-Korsakov's *Sadko*, Tchaikovsky's *Snow Maiden*. In addition, he was able to introduce the singer Chaliapin to Moscow audiences. His summer residence, Abramtsevo, near Moscow, was the main meeting-place of the leading painters, sculptors and musicians of his day and also became a centre of a native Russian craft revival. The murals of the chapel there were painted by his artist friends – Ilia Repin, N. M. Vasnetsov, V. D. Polenov, Serov, Korovin and Antakolsky.

Mamontov's end was not a happy one. In 1899 he was arrested for embezzling funds from the Moscow–Archangel Railway. He was found 'not guilty', but his creditors demanded a public auction of his private effects. His house, his art treasures, his beautiful furniture and rugs were all sold to meet their demands. He spent the remaining eighteen years of his life operating a small pottery studio in Moscow which again became a meeting-place for the intelligentsia of his day.

The great love of the theatre seems to have been a fairly common feature of the Russian merchant class. The classic example of this is, of course, the illustrious theatrical impresario Konstantin Stanislavsky, who was born into a merchant family. His father, he writes, was a rich manufacturer and merchant, the owner of a mercantile firm 100 years old. Every morning at six he used to make the train journey from his estate twenty miles outside Moscow into his city office, and then back again the same evening. This could have been the same house to which, late one evening, Stanislavsky took Nemirovich-Danchenko to discuss their plans for the Moscow Arts Theatre. It was a villa called 'Liubimovka', standing in a pine grove and with a little theatrical pavilion in its grounds. Everything in the main house was modest and durable, as was everything belonging to the mercantile class – the furniture, the silver plate, the linen – everything had that 'solid look'. Stanislavsky continued as a director of the Alexeiev family business concurrently with his theatrical enterprises for many years.

The generation of millionaire industrialists which followed continued the cultural tradition. The wealthy merchant Pavel Tretiakov worked from early morning till late at night in his office and factory. But every available moment left to him he spent amassing a collection of Russian paintings from the earliest beginnings of Russian art. His faith in his native art led him to make loans and subsidies to young artists and also to commission works for the gallery he built in the Transriver district of Moscow – the old merchant area, where he also lived. A bashful and timid man, his thin figure, with its bearded, priestlike face, was a frequent sight in European museums during the summer holiday period.

Another patron of the arts was Serge Shtchukin, who was one of the first people in the world to appreciate the work of contemporary French artists. He built up one of the largest collections of French paintings, including canvasses by Monet, Degas, Renoir, Gauguin, Cézanne, Van Gogh and, later, Matisse. Anyone who wanted to see the paintings was admitted free to the house. Serge's brother, Piotr, created a museum of Russian antiquities which was the first, though not the only, private museum in Russia.

Kosma T. Soldatenkov filled his beautiful Grecian-style house with books and fulfilled his debt to mankind by directing a publishing venture which produced only academic works unlikely to succeed in the commercial market. Bakrushin, yet another culturally-inclined merchant, founded the only museum of theatrical art in Russia. Baron Horace Guenzburg, son of Joseph Yevsel, was a generous patron of scientific, cultural and social institutions and of promising writers, artists and musicians. His house became a meeting-place for liberal intellectuals.

Savva Morozov is, however, the perfect example of the nine-

teenth- and twentieth-century Russian merchant–philanthropist. He never completely overcame his peasant origins, and his expensive European clothing hung awkwardly on his powerful body. He was endowed with tremendous energy and willpower. 'If anyone should stand in my way, I would ride right over him without blinking', he is quoted as saying, in his brusque voice and with his easy laugh. He was the leading representative of Moscow's merchant class, but, like Mamontov, half his vital energy was occupied with the Russian theatre. He was passionately in love with it and did, in fact, supply a major part of the finance for the Moscow Arts Theatre. He himself paid for the new building which he personally designed, and he spent lavishly on its equipment, which even included a revolving stage. He converted a bathroom in his own home into a laboratory, where he spent hours experimenting with paints and lacquers, smearing them on light bulbs to test their effects in

A Moscow businessman exhibits his philanthropic feelings. This picture seems strangely posed with its two lines of crippled beggars and the children on the bottom step, and could even have been taken for public relations purposes.

stage lighting. He was usually to be found back-stage on opening nights, dressed in working clothes and helping the mech-
anics and technicians. He was prepared to sit for hours on end
in restaurants, discussing his favourite topic, with nothing
before him but a bottle of Johannisberger, a glass of tea, or a
portion of ham.

Many of the major events in Moscow merchant and artistic
life took place in restaurants – possibly because the merchant
class rarely entertained formally at home. It is true, though,
that Bruce-Lockhart, appointed British Vice-Consul in Moscow
in 1912, was the guest of the Haritonenkos, the sugar kings of
Moscow, at a dinner given at their immense palace just opposite
the Kremlin, in honour of the British parliamentary delegation
visiting Russia in 1912. The whole house was a fairyland of
flowers brought from Nice, and orchestras seemed to be playing
in every ante-chamber. The evening began traditionally with
hot and cold *zakhouska*, served with vodka on long, narrow tables.
This was followed by an enormous meal which lasted until
11 p.m., followed, in its turn, by a ballet performed by some of

The entrance to one of
Moscow's famous
restaurants, the scene
of many an important
business deal.

Moscow's leading dancers: Geltzer, Mordkin and Balashova.
Even this did not mark the conclusion of the festivities. Still to
come was a violin recital of Chopin nocturnes by a leading per-
former, Sibor, and then the assembled company took to the
floor and danced. At four in the morning, a fleet of private
troikas arrived to take the guests on to the Strelna nightclub.

Most celebrations and large gatherings, however, took place
in restaurants, though it should be added that restaurants were
only for men and the *demi-monde*. The older generation did not
frequent them socially, and young married couples would dine
only in the private rooms. It was in the restaurant of the Hotel
Slavyansky Bazaar that Stanislavsky and Nemirovich-Danchenko had the famous interminable conversation that resulted
in the establishment of the Moscow Arts Theatre. More sober
than many of the other Moscow eating-places, its large handsome hall was full of financiers at 2 p.m., and the discussion
had to take place in a private room. All the really important
conferences of the Theatre shareholders, and many of its business meetings, were held at the more popular and showy
Hermitage Restaurant. Here, one chose one's *sterlet* from a
fishtank fountain, listened to the music of Krysh, the suave
Jewish violinist, and strolled in the beautifully laid-out summer
gardens. The surroundings were so attractive that some members of the theatrical profession used to spend a large part of
their lives there. Mikhail Provich Sadowsky used to stay there
for almost the whole day in the last years of his life, and even
received visitors there. The distinguished writer of *feuilletons*,
Doroshevich, also sat there for hours on end, writing when the
spirit moved him.

Bruce-Lockhart's first introduction to Moscow was the restaurant at the Metropole Hotel. 'I had entered a kingdom', he
wrote, 'where money was the only God.' His first impression
was of great wealth and crude coarseness – steaming furs, fat
women and big sleek men. The restaurant was a blaze of colour
and light. Along a balcony which ran round the main room were
brightly lit windows and doors leading into private rooms. The
restaurant itself was a maze of small tables, crowded with
'officers in badly-cut uniforms, Russian merchants with scented
beards, German commercial travellers with sallow complexions
and close-cropped heads' – and champagne everywhere. The
focal point of the room was the balustraded dais where an
orchestra, resplendent in red coats, played Viennese waltzes.

By himself, in a little pulpit, was the Czech violinist Konchik, the leader of the orchestra.

Testov's Tavern was more the home of merchant-Moscow. Here, they held their regular Tuesday dinners, noted for the gourmet quality of the food served. This was the time when important contacts were made and when anybody who had any standing in the business world had to put in an appearance. But the meals they were offered were ample compensation for the business element involved. Sucking pigs came straight from Testov's own farm; the treasurer of the club was a connoisseur of fruit drinks; but the *specialité de la maison* was the *kulibyaki* in a dozen layers, each layer composed of a different filling – meat, fish, mushrooms, chicken, game, etc. And all the while, Stepan Ryabov's orchestra played, and Hungarian and Russian gipsies sang. Afterwards, the men would invite the gipsy girls to their tables.

Gipsy-singing, the great love of every Russian, could also be heard at the Strelna, almost a palace with its glass roof and walls. The door was manned by a porter in braided uniform. Another servant took coats and galoshes. Then guests moved into the Palm Court, an immense, over-heated room where tropical plants proliferated in the middle of winter, and palm trees waved their fronds at ceiling level. The walls were surrounded by artificial caves, each holding little white tables at which the diners sat amid fountains playing into basins and waterfalls cascading down the sides of artificial rocks. The Palm Court led into a large pine-walled private room with a roaring wood fire in a vast open fireplace. When Bruce-Lockhart dined there, he sat at a large table near the fire and watched enchanted as Maria Nikolaievna entered, followed by eight gipsies, four men with guitars and four girls with 'eyes like sloes and sinuous graceful bodies'. They were all dressed in traditional gipsy costumes, the men in white-brocaded Russian shirts and coloured trousers, the girls in bright silk dresses and silk scarves around their heads. In repose, they looked mundane enough. When they sang, Bruce-Lockhart was moved to rhapsody:

This gipsy music [he wrote] is more intoxicating, more dangerous, than opium, or women, or drink, and, although champagne is a necessary adjunct to the enjoyment, there is a plaintiveness in its appeal which to the Slav and Celtic races is almost irresistible. For

better than words it expresses the pent-up and stifled desires of mankind. It induces a delicious melancholy which is half-lyrical, half-sensuous. Something there is in it of the boundless width of the Russian steppe. It is the uttermost antithesis of anything that is Anglo-Saxon. It breaks down all reserves of restraint. It will drive a man to the moneylenders and even to crime. . . .

Gipsies were an integral part of Russian folk myth. Engraving by Vall of a painting of a gipsy camp.

Native-born Russians could echo this eulogy. Prince Serge Obolensky in his youth frequented gipsy homes in the village of Novaya Derevynya in the Island district of St Petersburg. 'They could transcend the barest walls, warm the coldest calculating heart with their wizardry', he wrote. 'They were sheer hypnosis.'

In fact, no Russian 'party' was complete unless the gipsies were brought on. When Bruce-Lockhart treated himself to an evening out in Moscow, he first cashed a cheque at Muir and Mirrielees, the Harrods of the city. Then, after dining at the Hermitage, he went on to the Aquarium, a vast open-air amusement

park, presided over by a Negro called Thomas, to listen to the gipsies in one of the inevitable private rooms.

Moscow may have been the merchant city, but several ancient noble families still retained their estates in its vicinity, dating from the days when Moscow was still the political capital of Russia. Needless to say, the Youssoupovs were included in this group, with a magnificent *château* at Arkhangelskoie, where once the family ran a factory manufacturing exquisite crystal and porcelain. The *château* was reached by a long, straight avenue leading through a forest of pine trees and emerging into a circular courtyard surrounded by a colonnade. It had terraces all round, and an immense expanse of green lawn dotted with statues extended to the horizon. Within, the *château* resembled a museum. The downstairs halls were columned, the ceilings frescoed, and good pictures and statues adorned the walls and niches. Two rooms were, in fact, specially reserved for the works of Tiepolo and Hubert Robert. A library in the right wing contained 35,000 volumes, including 500 Elzevir editions and a Bible dating from 1462 in their original bindings, with bookplates inscribed '*ex Biblioteca Arkhangelina*'. The library was also graced by a life-sized mechanical model of Jean-Jacques Rousseau, in eighteenth-century French costume, seated at a table, which could be set in motion by the touch of a switch.

Another estate with its own factory was the Benckendorff property of Sosnovka in the province of Tambar, some 300 miles south-west of Moscow. Dark red paint manufactured there covered the whole of a timber house, except for the window frames. Built at the end of the eighteenth and the beginning of the nineteenth century, the only brick used in the construction was in the foundations and the cellars. About fifteen yards away from this dwelling was another two-storey house dating from the middle of the eighteenth century. This one was built of brick, L-shaped and painted white, with square brick columns picked out in bluish-grey. Both houses stood in a small park on the gentle slopes of a valley with a stream at the bottom, ending in a pool. The grounds were laid out very beautifully in avenues lined with lilac or lime trees, opening into a clearing where stood an old gnarled horse-chestnut tree encircled by benches. The flower gardens were a riot of Caucasian wild azaleas and

Some members of the aristocracy, too, had estates in the Moscow area. This is the Youssoupovs' *château* at Arkhangelskoie.

A *moujik* drives an elegant lady and her little girl into the country on a perfect summer day.

dwarf rhododendrons, with gentians for later flowering and tubs of orange trees brought from the Riviera. In late July and August the scene was particularly beautiful, when Indian convolvulus covered the red house right up to the roof with pale blue flowers. The gardens also contained a hot-house and quite extensive greenhouses which produced peaches, apricots and egg plums, while an enormous kitchen garden and an apple orchard of some twenty-five acres supplied more mundane needs. The estate naturally contained stables where eight carriage-horses, four riding-horses and several Kirghizian ponies were kept.

The Obolenskys also had a property in the Tambov district. It was called Ira and was used for extensive stock-rearing, with sheep, cattle and about 100 brood mares. The house itself was fantastic, built in the tradition of Russian rococo architecture. Panels of different colours covered the long frontage, giving the house a medieval chessboard effect, which was enhanced by the dome which rose above it. Inside all was peace, with great shaded rooms and long polished halls.

Most of the Obolensky property was in the district of Nizhny Novgorod, about 200 miles east of Moscow. Their estate of Krasnaya Gorka (Red Hill) consisted of 30,000 acres (the family altogether owned some 60,000 acres), with horses everywhere. The spacious, unpretentious brick house stood in a large park full of pine trees on a hill overlooking the River Imza. It had nine bedrooms in the main buildings, but the kitchens were built apart and stood alone some yards away.

Some of the nobility even had houses in Moscow itself. The Youssoupovs' house had been presented to the family by Peter II in the eighteenth century. Built by Ivan the Terrible in 1551, it was painted in bright colours in the old Muscovite style, and all the rooms were vaulted and decorated with frescoes. The largest room, which contained a collection of very fine gold and silver plate, was hung with portraits of the Tsars in carved frames.

5 The World of Art

Diaghilev and Stanislavsky, Nijinsky and Pavlova, Stravinsky and Scriabin, Gorki and Chaliapin, Benois and Bakst – rarely is such a galaxy of genius produced by one country at one time. Yet while *haute société* danced and chatted above the rumble of growing social discontent, and the Tsar and Tsarina sought refuge in tight family life and religious mysticism, the arts in Russia were enjoying a period of unprecedented activity. While the mass of Russia's population lived in illiteracy and ignorance, a great blossoming of creativity was giving rise to works which were wholly Russian and yet totally remote from the Russian nation as a whole. Never had the gap between people and culture been so great.

After the Russian defeat of 1905 the intelligentsia, disillusioned and disenchanted, spent the following decade in flight from reality, finding refuge in individualism, symbolism and religious yearnings. Never before had so many talents competed to express themselves through artistic media, never had there been so large an élite of intellectuals, of people informed and enthusiastic about the arts. To quote the philosopher Nicholas Berdiaev, it seemed as if creativity were the only means whereby the human spirit could free itself from the prison of ordinary life. The free and beautiful cosmos of art seemed to offer new possibilities for harmonizing the discords of an increasingly disturbed world.

Under the inspiration of a few exceptionally gifted individuals, the Russian arts broke free of all confinements. They no longer restricted themselves to one form, one city or one country. They merged together, so that the ballet, for example, was no longer limited to the art of the dancer but became a blend of the creativity of composer and choreographer, artist and dancer. The foremost painters of the day designed backcloths and costumes for theatre and ballet. One art flowed into another. Futurism began in painting and moved into poetry. The painter Vrubel drew much of the inspiration for his passionate religious paintings from the poets, and his florid colours, in their turn, inspired other poets such as the Symbolist Alexander Blok. Futurist poets and painters met to exchange ideas at 'The Nest of Music', David Burlink's Moscow home. The Russian creative artist drew on Russia's past and adapted it to the mood of the future; symptomatic of this was the opening in Moscow in 1913 of the first large exhibition of fully restored ancient ikons. Works by Russian artists were taken out of the artistic capitals of the

PREVIOUS PAGES
Benois's decor for the ballet *Le Pavillon d'Armide*.

OPPOSITE Three giants of Russian literature – on the right is the ageing Tolstoy, next to him Chekov, and standing behind them is Gorki.

III

country to the country at large. Alexander Scriabin, one of the greatest pianists and most original composers of the epoch, staged innumerable exhibitions, concerts and cultural tours through provincial Russia, including performances on a barge sailing down the Volga. In 1913, the 'Futurist tour' by *avant-garde* poets and painters visited seventeen provincial cities. The world of Russian art opened itself to European influence: collections of contemporary French art were amassed and exhibitions held. Conversely, the Russian arts were exported. A previous generation of geniuses, Tolstoy and Dostoyevsky, Tchaikovsky and Rimsky-Korsakov, had already proved to the West that they were capable of competing with, if not instructing, European artists. Now, Konstantin Serge Stanislavsky took his Moscow Arts Theatre Company to Europe to confirm the fact. Serge Diaghilev's Ballets Russes never played to Russian audiences at all; though intensely Russian in origin, they were solely a dazzling feature of the European and American cultural scenes. In 1913, Paris heard the first performance of Stravinsky's ultra-modern, neo-pagan *Rite of Spring* – and Stravinsky's work itself was a blend of the newest Western polytonal and polyrhythmic ideas and Russian themes.

An English writer, Stephen Graham, who arrived in Russia in January 1914, was from the first struck by the cultural ferment he was entering. 'The Futurists', he was told, 'are walking about with gilded noses and dyed faces. . . . Everyone has been discussing a play of Artsybashev called *Jealousy*. Literary Russia has been giving a welcome to the Belgian poet Verhaeren, such as you in England have been giving Anatole France. Everyone is either hearing or giving lectures about Verhaeren. But I suppose most clamour of all has been aroused about Gorki and Dostoyevsky and the Theatre of Art at Moscow. . . .'

The Moscow Arts Theatre, under Konstantin Stanislavsky and Vladimir Nemirovich-Danchenko, was by 1914 the leading theatre of Russia – if not of the whole world. It had originally been started in 1898, in the vast wave of creativity that struck the Russian cultural world at the end of the nineteenth century and the beginning of the twentieth, as an attempt to reform the Russian theatre and make it more realistic. Costumes, stage sets, music and sound were all brought into play to enhance the realism of the drama and the mood created by the actors. The smallest detail of the production was handled with the same concern for realism. When historical plays were produced, the costumes were copied exactly from the period concerned, after conscientious research in museums and art galleries, and the actors were obliged to wear them for a long time before the performance, in order to become as accustomed to moving in them as in their own everyday clothes. In rural scenes, real trees replaced the painted backcloth. In interiors, rooms had real walls, real ceilings and real windows. Real food was served on the real table, and real tea was poured from real samovars. Real fires were kindled in real grates. All in all, the audience was given the impression of looking in at the intimate life of the characters portrayed. In Tolstoy's *Tsar Feodor*, for example, the audience was thrown headlong into a noisy boyar feast. Servants ran to and fro across the stage, rolling kegs of wine, bearing vast plates laden with roasted geese and pigs and heaped with fruit and vegetables.

Stanislavsky's ideas gradually evolved as the years advanced, to mirror the Symbolist and Futurist trends prevalent in the period before the First World War. From believing that realism

Stanislavsky in his own 1911 Moscow Arts Theatre production of Turgenev's comedy *The Lady from the Provinces.*

should be an end in itself, he came to think that naturalness should be only the tool of drama. The end was a spiritual state,

just as it was shown by Modernistic painters on their canvases, by the musicians of the new school in their compositions, and by new poets in their poetry. The works of these painters, musicians and poets have no clear outline, no definite and finished melodies, no clear thoughts. The strength of these works lies in the combination of blending of colours, lines, musical notes and the euphony of words. They create a mood that subconsciously infects the audience. They give hints which compel the spectator to create a picture in his own imagination.

Stanislavsky demanded – and received – complete dedication from the company he gathered around him, and which he rehearsed for long periods before each production on an estate in the country. He also felt it necessary to enforce an unusual discipline on the audience he entertained. Once the curtain had risen promptly at eight o'clock, no one was allowed to enter the theatre until the first act had ended. Absolute silence was essential so that the subtle sound effects could be fully appreciated: the whisper of the wind, the distant clip-clop of horses' hooves approaching from afar, even the chirping of crickets. Rumour had it that Stanislavsky bred crickets purely for this purpose on one of his country estates. The design of the theatre itself was specifically calculated not to distract one iota from the interest of the production. The Moscow Arts Theatre was a model of simplicity. Walls and stalls were pure, matt grey and the curtain, also grey, was decorated with only a simple representation of a white seagull – a symbol of Chekov's *Seagull*, one of the theatre's greatest triumphs.

Stanislavsky and his Moscow Arts Theatre illustrate many of the trends typical of the period. His methods had a profound influence on the European and American stage for years to come. His productions scored resounding triumphs in Western capitals, particularly Berlin, where the Kaiser was among the audience. And the company brought to the fore new talents: actors and actresses, such as Ivan Moskvin, Vera Komissarzhevskaya and Olga Knipper (Chekov's wife); such directors as Vsevolod Meyerhold and Eugene Vakhtangov; and musicians, such as Alexander Gretchaninov. And it provided a stage for the two great Russian writers of the first decade of the twentieth century: Anton Chekov and Maxim Gorki.

Maxim Gorki's brilliant portrayals of poverty and low life made him the first major writer of post-revolutionary Russia. Chekov first introduced him to Russian literary life at the end of the nineteenth century.

Gorki, author of the revolution and of the depths of the Russian soul, was himself in the audience at the Arts Theatre on the March evening when Stephen Graham went to see Nemirovich-Danchenko's adaptation of Dostoyevsky's *The Possessed*, re-entitled *Nikolai Stavrogin*. Gorki, back in Russia after an absence of eight years, had his hair cut short, Graham noted. He was wearing a European jacket, waistcoat and collar, and light evening boots. His health did not seem too bad, although it was purportedly his health which had kept him from his native land, but his face was nervous and self-conscious. It was not by any means the old Gorki who had returned.

Yet Gorki at that moment was the centre of a controversy which was buzzing through the literary and intellectual circles of Moscow. And the play that both he and Graham were watching – a play dominated by a sense of truly Russian failure – was the immediate cause of the innumerable meetings that had been held and the letters that had appeared in the Press before its production. Even the great artist Alexander Benois had been brought from St Petersburg to join in the controversy.

It had begun with an open letter by Gorki written from Capri which appeared in one of the most widely-read newspapers, *Russkoye Slovo*, protesting at the production of Dostoyevsky at such a juncture in the country's history. A later letter published in the Press explained:

I know the frailty of the Russian character, I know the compassionate wavering of the Russian soul and its tendency, in its torment, weariness and despair, towards all contagions. . . . Not *Stavrogin* should be shown it now, but something quite different. It should be exhorted to boldness, spiritual health, activity and not introspection; it should be exhorted to return to the source of energy – to democracy, to the people, to sociableness and to science.

The Theatre – and most of the Press, including Mereshkovsky, writing in the *Russian Word*, supported it – based its justification on the 'higher probings of the soul' and argued that it had joined art to science and social consciousness and regarded it as the source of energy for healthy activity. '. . . The frail soul of *Uncle Vanya*, and the introspection of *Hamlet*, and the *Symphonie Pathétique* of Tchaikovsky – it all depended on how it was done', writes Nemirovich-Danchenko in his autobiography. Later, in 1934, at the first Congress of Soviet Writers, Gorki was still to claim that 'The main and basic theme of pre-revolutionary literature was the tragedy of a person to whom life seemed cramped, who felt superfluous in society, sought therein a comfortable place, failed to find it and suffered, died or reconciled himself to a society that was hostile to him, or sank to drunkenness or suicide.'

Whichever of the protagonists was right, the public had certainly taken the Moscow Arts Theatre to its heart. Crowds thronged there nightly to see the curtain rise on the small village church scene with which *Nikolai Stavrogin* opened, or *The*

Mistress of the Inn, or *Thought* by Leonid Andreev, in those early months of 1914. Afterwards, when the final curtain had fallen half an hour after midnight, they would stagger out, dazed, and move on, perhaps to the 'Bat', the favourite haunt of literary and artistic Moscow, where cabaret performances began when the Moscow Arts had finished. It had, in fact, been started as a sort of club for the Theatre on 29 February 1908, in the small, comfortable but poor cellar of a house near the Temple of the Saviour. It was a place where the artist could relax after the tensions of his work, where he could drink a cup of coffee or a glass of wine and chat with his friends, or where, if he had a hidden desire to act in cabaret, he could indulge this whim. Two such men, Nikolai Tarassov and his friend Nikita Baliev, who excelled in such diversions as cabaret demanded, were prominent in establishing the 'Bat'. Moscow was enchanted by it – all the more so as it was not easy to gain admittance, and the satire, burlesques and grotesques which formed its programme were formerly quite unknown to the city. Many actors and actresses still went there to dine as well as to see the performance, and Gorki and the great singer Feodor Chaliapin were amongst its *habitués*.

In contrast to Stanislavsky and his production of Dostoyevsky, another play of a completely different *genre* was also attracting considerable attention at the same period. Stephen Graham went to see *Jealousy* when it was performed in Kiev and commented that it was enjoying a 'vulgar success'. But this was nothing compared with the success its author, Michael Artsybashev, had gained over the preceding ten years. In complete opposition to the pure and idealistic aims of the great artistic movements, his works reflected the needs of the growing middle class in Russia, fed by her increasing industrialization, for a more earthy type of entertainment. They concentrated on sexual problems and the male–female relationship. They reflected the life of people whose sole ambition was to make money, whose sole goal was physical satisfaction and whose relaxation was feasting and flirtation. *Jealousy* was no exception. It basically constituted, Graham tells us, a public trial of woman, and told the story of a husband whose wife was addicted to flirting even though she loved him dearly. In the end, the husband, driven beyond endurance, strangled her, and the audience was given pencil and paper and asked to state whether his action was justified. In Kiev, *Jealousy* was playing to packed houses –

though Graham noticed a difference between the audience there and in the capitals. No one wore evening dress in the provincial theatre, although he noted that many of the women were somewhat pretentiously garbed. There were many rich townsfolk in the stalls, while clerks escorting wives or sweethearts were scattered over the rest of the house.

Artsybashev was not alone in his disillusion and morbidity. A whole cult of sex and suicide had grown up. As early as 1907 the two bestselling novels had been his *Sanine* and Feodor Sologub's *The Petty Demon*, while Leonid Andreev's pictures of syphilis and suicide in *The Abyss* and *In the Fog*, and Alexander Kuprin's panorama of urban prostitution in *The Pit* continued the tradition. Andreev attained considerable success as a playwright and was one of the most popular dramatists in the years between 1907 and 1914.

The Russian public flocked to the theatre, and Stephen Graham took full advantage of the opportunities the Russian drama offered. In March 1914 he was spellbound by the production at Moscow's Free Theatre of Gogol's *Fair of Sorotchinsky*. The producer Mardjanov had, he thought, excelled himself in re-creating the authentic atmosphere of the Russian crowd. Each detail, each minor part, was portrayed with meticulous accuracy. All the bustle, talking, bargaining and singing were allowed to mingle with the action of the play. People, peasants, storekeepers and beggars moved in and out of the stalls. The audience was transported body and soul to the fair.

Mardjanov may or may not have been a follower of Stanislavsky in his realism. But Stanislavsky in the last years before the war was no longer in the *avant garde*. In 1912, a crowd of young men and women from his own Moscow Arts Theatre gathered in a small place in Tverskaya Street, which was later called The First Studio of the Moscow Arts Theatre. They opened in January 1913 with *The Shipwreck of 'Hope'* by a Dutch playwright, Herman Heyermans. Benois, Stanislavsky and Nemirovich-Danchenko were in the audience. The studio went from strength to strength. It presented 1914 with what was possibly its most spectacular theatrical event, in its production of *The Cricket on the Hearth*.

The year 1914 saw the establishment of another innovation: the Kamerny (Chamber) Theatre, founded by Alexander Tairov, who was profoundly opposed to Stanislavsky's emphasis on realism. With his 'expressive gesture' technique, built on the assumption that the actor could convey emotion mainly with his body, that gait and movement were more important than speech, he had massive plans for breaking new ground. He opened with *Sakuntala*, by the great Sanskrit poet Kalidasa, adapted by the Russian Symbolist poet Konstantin Dimitryevich Balmont, filling his stage on this occasion with half-naked bodies. He employed another poet, the Lithuanian Jurgii Kazimirovich Baltrushaytis, as literary adviser to the scheme, and commissioned Boris Pasternak to translate Kleist's comedy *The Broken Jug*.

While Moscow attained the greater reputation as the home of the Russian theatre – possibly because of the prominence achieved by Stanislavsky – the St Petersburg stage was experiencing a parallel development. In fact St Petersburg was the scene of one of the earliest and most important experimental ventures. In 1904 the talented actress Vera Komissarzhevskaya opened her own theatre in the capital. Two years later she engaged Vsevolod Meyerhold as director and moved to premises in Officers' Street – which rapidly became a lively centre for Symbolist writers, Modernist painters and *avant garde* composers. They flocked not only to all its productions but also to the Sunday evening recitals of poetry and music. Meyerhold now had a free hand to put his ideas of non-realistic theatre into practice and succeeded admirably with his first production at Officers' Street – equipped with a new curtain designed by Bakst, depicting a Greek temple and a sphinx. His *Hedda Gabler* was built on the idea of the correspondence between moods and colours, so dear to the hearts of the French Symbolists. Each character had his own colour. A contemporary account of the final effect states that

The stage seemed filled with bluish-green-silver mist. The background was blue. On the right side, a huge transom, the whole height of the stage, represented a window. Underneath stuck out the leaves of a black rhododendron. Outside the window, the air was greenish-blue. In the last act, the twinkling of stars pierced the bluish mist. On the left, the whole wall was occupied by a huge tapestry representing a silvery-gold woman with a deer. Silver lace decorated the top and the wings of the stage. Greenish-blue carpet covered the floor. The furniture, including a grand piano, was white. Green-white vases held large white chrysanthemums. White furs were thrown over a strangely-shaped sofa on which Hedda reclined – in a sea-watery green dress. It shimmered and flowed at her every movement, and she resembled a sea serpent with shiny scales.

There was no end to Meyerhold's experiments in utilizing the theatre as a means of conveying purified extracts of emotion, purged of naturalistic vestiges. One of his most interesting ventures, however, was to stage a series of poetic dramas by the great Symbolist poet Alexander Blok.

Vera Komissarzhevskaya's theatre was forced to close in 1909, and shortly afterwards Meyerhold moved on to take up employment with the Imperial Alexandrinsky Theatre. He had changed his interest by this time and was more concerned with obtaining a union of actor and spectator in a revelry of light, colour and movement, greatly assisted in this respect by the designs created by Alexander Golovin for his luxurious settings.

Another opponent of theatrical realism was Nikolai Evreinov who opened his Ancient Theatre in St Petersburg in 1907. Evreinov also ran a 'theatre of smaller forms', known as 'The Crooked Mirror', a parallel development to Moscow's 'Bat'. There were other St Petersburg venues where artistes from leading theatres could dine after the shows and perhaps improvise performances for the delight of the writers, poets and painters who gathered – at the Stray Dog in a cellar on Mikhailovsky Street, for example, or the Comedians' Inn.

It was the intellectual elite who frequented these experimental ventures. More popular, by definition, was the Narodny Dom, the 'House of the People' which Nicholas II had founded in 1901. It was an enormous building behind the Petropavlovsk Fortress on the bank of the Kronversky Canal, housing not only a theatre but also concert rooms, cinemas and restaurants. The architecture was entirely functional and directed towards providing a place where the lower orders could procure entertainment at a minimal cost. Although only a few boxes and several rows of stalls were available at a higher price for the more wealthy and although it was not the custom to 'dress' to attend performances, it had become a fashionable centre both for the higher echelons of society and for leading artistes. Chaliapin made frequent appearances in opera there, and there it was that Diaghilev's ballet company in 1911 obtained its one and only engagement on Russian soil (in the event it never performed there; a fire in the theatre forced a cancellation).

St Petersburg was renowned as the home of the ballet. Here, every Sunday and Wednesday evening from September to Lent, the fashionable world, resplendent in furs and diamonds or gorgeous uniforms, moved towards the Maryinsky Theatre to

If Moscow was the home of the theatre, St Petersburg was the balletomane's Mecca. Mathilde Kschessinska in the 1911 production of *Le Pavillon d'Armide*.

see the Imperial Ballet Company at its work. Interest in the ballet had become immense, and the theatre was filled nightly with solid blocks of balletomanes, reluctant to miss a single performance. The well-to-do were regular subscribers to permanent seats in the stalls or to boxes. Competition to obtain one of these seats was intense, and a new face in the ranks caused a veritable flurry among the old. They were a discerning and critical audience, these balletomanes, suspicious of innovation, ready to note and assess any change, however minor, in a performance. They had their favourites too; it was an acknowledged fact that when the prima ballerina Mathilde Kschessinska danced in Moscow, the front row of the Maryinsky was completely empty. The gallery and pit were filled with more impoverished balletomanes – students in elegant cloaks, schoolboys in the grey overcoats of their uniform, who gave vent to their enthusiasm in no uncertain terms. When the performance was ended, they rushed to jostle and push round the narrow stage-door in an attempt to greet the artistes in person.

A veritable cult surrounded the ballerinas of the imperial theatres. They were trained from the age of nine at the Imperial Ballet Schools to a life of complete devotion to their art. They emerged as civil servants, in that the state which owned and maintained both theatre and ballet school paid their salaries. But their profession gave them a position in society independent of all class and the opportunity of mingling with the most exalted. Mathilde Kschessinska was the mistress of Nicholas II before he acceded to the throne. When, as happened on more than one occasion, she felt herself unjustly treated by the administration, she appealed personally to the Tsar. In 1901, for example, when she was fined for refusing to wear hoop petticoats under her costume in *La Camargo*, she wrote to the Tsar. The fine was rescinded, and the Director of the Imperial Theatre resigned.

The jewels and possessions these ballerinas accumulated were second to none. Kschessinska drew up an inventory of the gifts she received on 13 February 1911, when she celebrated twenty years of dancing on the imperial stage. They included a mahogany chest with gold banding containing a collection of yellow diamonds of all sizes, a large elephant made out of a pink precious stone with ruby eyes, an enamel powder-case on a gold frame, a green malachite table with a silver rim, a diamond watch with a diamond and platinum chain, a Louis XV mirror in a silver setting, and a silver flower vase. And this is not to mention the Tsar's own present of an outstretched diamond eagle mounted in platinum and with a platinum chain; under the eagle hung a rose sapphire set in diamonds. Her lover the Grand Duke Andrei went even further, buying her a diadem with diamonds and sapphires from Fabergé, similar to the gilt diadem she wore in *La Fille du Pharaon*. When she wore this piece to dinner at the Savoy Hotel one evening in London, the management insisted that two plain-clothes policemen dine at a neighbouring table.

In 1913 the season opened as it always did, on the first Sunday in September. Michael Fokine was the official ballet-master at the Maryinsky. The general revolution which had affected all

Fokine, ballet-master
at the Maryinsky
Theatre and a great
innovator in the world of
dance. Drawing by
V. Serov, 1912.

the arts in Russia at the end of the nineteenth century and the
beginning of the twentieth had swept through the ballet too. It
had coincided with the emergence of a host of great dancers, a
sudden blossoming of genius. Within the space of a few years,
dancers such as Anna Pavlova, Tamara Karsavina and Vaslav
Nijinsky all graduated from the Imperial Ballet School. Fokine
could not have wished for more exciting performers to carry out
his new ideas. Influenced by Isadora Duncan, the American
dancer who caused a sensation in St Petersburg in 1905, he

embarked on a policy of combining her ideas of dance as a completely natural means of expression with the old classical ballet preserved in static form by his predecessor, Marius Petipa. Essential to the revised art form that he introduced was his first major tenet: that 'music is not the mere accompaniment of a rhythmic step but an organic part of a dance; the quality of choreographic inspiration is determined by the quality of the music.' By clearing classical ballet of its frontage of rhetoric, ready-made formulae, mimetic monologues and fixed poems, and replacing them by theme, atmosphere and correct style, he brought its technique forward to new glories.

For his ballet *Eunice*, based on Sienkiewicz's *Quo Vadis*, he did a vast amount of research in the Hermitage Museum into classical dances depicted on Greek and Roman vases, so that he could capture the true spirit of the period. Ridiculed at its first performance on 10 December 1906, when both Kschessinska and Pavlova danced, by the season of 1913–14 Fokine's methods were in general acceptance at the Maryinsky. In fact by that date the ballets he was presenting there had, like the Moscow Arts Theatre, come to be accepted as 'traditional'. On 2 February 1914, for example, Mathilde Kschessinska danced a new production by Nicholas Legat of *Le Talisman* by Drigo, at a benefit performance for the *corps de ballet*. A week later she played Esmeralda with N. Legat in another benefit performance, this time to celebrate the twenty-fifth anniversary of Legat's entry into the Imperial Theatre. Nicholas II was in the imperial box on that occasion, and this gave particular significance to Kschessinska's performance of a part she had first danced in 1899. It contains a famous jealousy scene in which Esmeralda has to dance a *pas-de-deux* before her lover and her fiancé. We do not know if the Tsar attached any importance to this event. To Kschessinska it meant a great deal. She refused to dance *Sleeping Beauty* the following Sunday. 'In spite of my desire to dance again in the presence of the Tsar,' she writes, '. . . I wanted to leave him with the impression of Esmeralda.'

The search for new means of expression in the art was centred in another company. The Maryinsky was now the 'establishment'. It was Diaghilev's Ballets Russes – an independent company – that were responsible for the innovations and experiments in ballet techniques in the years preceding the First World War.

Serge Pavlovich Diaghilev was perhaps the greatest innovator of them all, the man most directly responsible for the great

Diaghilev, creator of the Ballets Russes and the inspiration behind the tremendous flowering of the arts in turn-of-the-century Russia.

Chaliapin in the title role of Mussorgsky's opera *Boris Godunov*.

blossoming of all Russian arts at the turn of the century. He began his personal revolution in the field of the visual arts, founding a movement and a journal called *The World of Art*, aimed at purifying art from the decadence and utilitarian elements that had pervaded it in the nineteenth century. Diaghilev was looking for new paths and new formulae, removed from traditional standards and accepted canons. He preached a cult of personality based on the fundamental principle that art must express the artist's individuality. '. . . The importance and significance of a work of art', he wrote, 'lies in how clearly and how sharply it defines the personality of its creator, and the degree to

which it establishes contact with the personality of the beholder.'
While still engaged in encouraging art within Russia, it was he
who accomplished so much in the way of introducing European
art to Russia, Russian art to Europe, and Russian art to the
Russian people at large, organizing important exhibitions in
every direction. In 1908 he went a step further and took Mussorgsky's opera *Boris Godunov* to Paris, with Chaliapin in the
title role. Kschessinska was actually in the theatre on that unfor-
gettable night. The reception which the production received
was, she tells us, indescribable. The public were carried away
by Chaliapin's acting and singing. The ovation as the final curtain
fell was deafening.

One of Diaghilev's greatest merits was his ability to bring
together groups of artists in productive collaboration, and he
was joined in these activities by many like-minded individuals,
among them the great artists Alexander Benois and Léon Bakst.
Bakst was a fellow-guest round the oval tea-table in the small
dining-room on the day Serge Grigoriev, future royal *régisseur*
of the Ballets Russes, first visited Diaghilev's apartment in St
Petersburg, the hearth of his great ventures. Grigoriev was
struck by Bakst's carefully brushed, curly red hair and his lively,
half-laughing eyes. He was clean-shaven and elegantly dressed,
smelled of perfume and spoke with a curious accent, giving his
'Rs' a guttural pronunciation; Diaghilev affectionately called him
'Lyóvushka'. Bakst, to the ballerina Tamara Karsavina, symbolized the exotic, the fantastic, the spice and sombreness of the
East and the serene aloofness of classical antiquity. Benois, on
the other hand, was a more subdued character, a blend of
inspiration and clear thought, wisdom and practicability.
Karsavina found him overflowing with benignity. His erudition
was unique, and his mastery of combining the fantastic with the
real was enhanced by the simplicity of the means he employed.
Both Benois and Bakst were highly talented artists. Benois's
landscapes are sometimes numbered among the finest paintings
of modern times. Both turned their attention at this period to
designing décor for theatre and ballet.

These were two of the men at Diaghilev's table. But everything in that apartment was of interest to Grigoriev. Not that
it was an artistic showplace in itself – all its contents were
simple and severe. There were only three or four good pictures
on the wide-striped wallpaper of the salon. There was an open
grand piano with music on it. A large Delft vase containing

flowers stood on a table. Above the door was a death-mask of
Beethoven. Grigoriev even recalled the food that was served on
that first afternoon: biscuits and jam and several plates of
Russian sweets. On Diaghilev's right stood a samovar from which
his valet, Vasili, poured tea.

Of no less interest was the appearance of Diaghilev himself.
He was a tall and rather thick-set man, with a large head and an
interesting face. He had a small black moustache and thick
dark hair with a heavy white streak on the right temple which
earned him the nickname 'Chinchilla'.

Diaghilev had gradually turned his attention to the ballet,
which seemed to him to offer the perfect blend of all the arts –
music, dancing and painting. He worked for a brief period with
the Imperial Ballet Company, but a break was not long in coming,
and he formed his own troupe. He took ballets with backcloths
designed by Benois and Bakst, to music specially composed by
Stravinsky, with choreography by Fokine or Nijinsky, to Paris
and London (where the company was amused to find an opera
house in the middle of a fruit market), Monte Carlo and Vienna,
Berlin and Dresden. The topmost artistes from the Maryinsky,
Fokine himself, Kschessinska, Karsavina, Pavlova and, of

Anna Pavlova,
exquisite as the dying
swan.

course, Vaslav Nijinsky, joined Diaghilev when their engage-
ments with the Imperial Theatre Company permitted. Nijinsky,
in fact, was able to take up full-time employment with Diaghilev
after he was dismissed from the Imperial Theatre in 1911. He
had refused to wear the regulation trunks under the costume
designed by Benois, which, a contemporary observer commented, displayed his figure a little too distinctly when he danced
in *Giselle* at the Maryinsky. Rumour had it that the Dowager
Empress, who was in the audience that evening, had found his
appearance indecent, but the official version of the expulsion
based it on Nijinsky's insubordination.

Diaghilev first introduced the Parisian public to Russian ballet
in 1909, when he took over a mixed programme of opera and
ballet. Paris was enthralled. This is hardly surprising, as
Parisians were able, among many other pleasures, to see Pavlova,
romantic, ethereal and unearthly, dancing a Sylphide to
Nijinsky's young poet. Benois's décor, combined with the
superb dancing, created a dream of poetic beauty, and Nijinsky's
leap, when he seemed to rise in the air and float into the wings,
made ballet history. In fact, the attention focused on Nijinsky
began a revolution in ballet generally, giving male dancing a new
direction and style.

To all Diaghilev's other talents, he added a genius for dis-
covering and utilizing potential abilities in others. The group
around his dining-table shuddered when he announced to them
in 1910 that he had commissioned a young composer to provide
the score for a new ballet, the *Firebird*. It was all right, Diaghilev
assured them. He had heard one piece by this composer, called
Fireworks, played at a concert at the Academy of Music. Half
the members of the circle had never heard of Igor Stravinsky
at that time, except perhaps as a young man of promise. When
the score of *Firebird*, a ballet based on a Russian fairytale, was
delivered, the dancers were dismayed by its absence of melody.

Stravinsky, a rather short man with prominent features and a very serious expression, had to be present at most of the rehearsals, banging out the tempo and rhythms on the piano to explain them to the dancers. In the event, *Firebird* was a tremendous success when it opened in Paris in 1910, with Karsavina, noble and imperious, in the title role, and from that moment Stravinsky became a regular member of Diaghilev's group.

The same season saw another Diaghilev triumph. The ballet *Shéhérazade* was a perfect example of the heights that co-operation between artist, composer and dancer could achieve. The décor by Bakst was a symphony of greenish-blues, with an orange stage cloth; Fokine's choreography reached unprecedented standards of excellence, Nijinsky danced the Negro superbly, and the music by Rimsky-Korsakov was sheer delight.

Diaghilev's ability to appreciate unidentified talent was never better demonstrated than in 1913. In that year a totally unexpected vacancy occurred in his company: Nijinsky had been dismissed. While on a tour of South America, the dancer had, much to everyone's surprise, married a young ballerina. He had also refused to appear with the company at one performance. This was a breach of contract which Diaghilev could not countenance. Nijinsky was dismissed. At first he seemed irreplaceable. Yet in 1914 Diaghilev was able to announce that he had signed a long-term contract with a young dancer he had spotted at the Bolshoi Theatre, Moscow. 'Of course he's rather provincial, but we'll soon put an end to that. His name is Massine. . . .' Leonid Massine made his début with the company in Paris on 17 May 1914, dancing Joseph in *La Légende de Joseph* for which music had been specially composed by Richard Strauss.

In the years before the breach with Nijinsky, Diaghilev had been encouraging him to work not only as a dancer but as a choreographer too. This had resulted in three Futurist ballets which mirrored the contemporary trend in the arts generally. *L'Après-Midi d'un Faune* was the first of these. Against a backcloth by Bakst depicting a tree-fringed lake, a very simple story was enacted. Some nymphs, clad in pleated Greek tunics of thin gauze and wearing stylized wigs, come to bathe. They are unaware of the fact that they are being watched by a faun. When he appears, they run off in horror. But one of them drops her veil in her haste. The faun picks it up and falls upon it in a frenzy of

"L'APRÈS-MIDI D'UN FAUNE"
(NIJINSKY)

7ᵐᵉ Saison
des
Ballets
Russes

BAKST

NIJINSKI, dans l'"Après-Midi d'un Faune"
Aquarelle originale de Léon Bakst.

love. When Nijinsky danced the faun on the opening night, 21 May 1912, the Parisian public raised an outraged protest on the grounds that the ballet was sexually offensive and Nijinsky's final pose indecent. But this was not the sole reason for the ballet's early unpopularity. The choreography marked a sharp break with traditional technique. Nijinsky's aim had been to bring to life an archaic Greek *bas-relief*. To produce this effect, he made the dancers move rhythmically to the music and then stop and hold the attitudes they were caught in. They had to move with bent knees and feet placed flat on the ground, heel first. They also had to keep their heads in profile while still making their bodies face the audience and to hold their arms rigid in various angular positions. Debussy's impressionistic music did nothing to facilitate these primitive evolutions.

One day, when I was finishing the last pages of *L'Oiseau de Feu* in St Petersburg, I had a fleeting vision which came to me as a complete surprise, my mind at the moment being full of other things [wrote Stravinsky in his memoirs]. I saw in imagination a solemn pagan rite: sage elders, seated in a circle, watched a young girl dance herself to death. They were sacrificing her to propitiate the god of spring. . . . I must confess that this vision made a deep impression on me, and I at once described it to my friend Nicholas Roerich, he being a painter who had specialized in pagan subjects. He welcomed my inspiration with enthusiasm and became my collaborator in this creation. I told Diaghilev about it, and he was at once carried away by the idea. . . .

So was born *Le Sacré du Printemps*, which in 1913 caused an even greater sensation than *L'Après-Midi*. Nijinsky's aim was to present a succession of rhythmically moving groups representing a series of primitive rites. Stravinsky's music, full of constantly changing rhythms, was indescribably difficult for the dancers. However, on the first night in Paris this music was barely heard. It was drowned by the shouting in the auditorium where fighting broke out.

Stravinsky recorded his reaction from the wings:

As I left the auditorium at the first bars of the prelude, which had at once evoked derisive laughter, I was disgusted. These demonstrations, at first isolated, soon became general, provoking counter-demonstrations and very quickly developing into a terrific uproar. During the whole performance I was at Nijinsky's side in the wings. He was standing on a chair, screaming 'sixteen, seventeen, eighteen'

– they had their own method of counting to keep time. Naturally the poor dancers could hear nothing by reason of the row in the auditorium and the sound of their own dance-steps. I had to hold Nijinsky by his clothes, for he was furious and ready to dash on to the stage at any moment and create a scandal. Diaghilev kept ordering the electricians to turn the lights on and off, hoping in that way to put a stop to the noise. . . .

Jeux, a tennis ballet to music by Debussy and décor by Bakst, was merely met with blank incomprehension. Audiences accustomed to the gentle, mellifluous beauty of classical ballet were unable to stomach the sharp, jerky, deliberately unbeautiful movements in which Nijinsky sought to express contemporary trends. Even the ballerinas found it difficult to understand what was required of them. Karsavina explains how she had to keep her head screwed on one side and both hands curled in as if she were maimed from birth.

The Futurists were certainly a colourful and active element in the 1914 Russian scene. They were also, with their complete denial of the past, rapidly becoming the dominant intellectual group. They rejected the mysticism and aestheticism of the prevalent Symbolist movement, were attracted by the technological aspects of modern life and propagated their views in 1912 in a manifesto, *A Slap in the Face of Public Taste*. They took a delight in bizarre clothing and walked about the town with abstract signs painted on their cheeks, and radishes in their buttonholes. Particularly picturesque were the Burlink brothers who organized a Futurist tour in 1913–14. Painter-poets by vocation, the younger brother, Vladimir, was a professional wrestler and was always seen carrying enormous weights wherever he was. David, a gigantic figure of a man, had 'I am Burlink' painted on his forehead. The Burlinks were also involved in a Futurist film, *Drama in Cabaret 13*, made towards the end of 1913 and depicting an average bawdy day in the lives of the Futurists. The artists themselves – the Burlinks, Maiakovsky, the most outstanding figure in Russian Futurism, Larionov and others – acted in the film, which satirized everything – the film industry, the society that patronized it and the entire subject of sex through which one senseless generation produced the next. December 1913 also saw the designs for a Futurist opera, *Victory Over the Sun*, in which characters were transformed into moving machines by cardboard-and-wire costumes designed by the artist Malevich, in which some of the

A few clever lines from the observant Cocteau's pen show Diaghilev as the egocentric genius who demanded absolute obedience and loyalty from his dancers and choreographers.

135

actors spoke only in vowels, some only in consonants, and in which blinding lights and ear-splitting sounds rent the theatre, all in an effort to give man freedom from dependence on the traditional order as symbolized by victory over the sun.

Young people in their numbers belonged to the new artistic movements. There was the 'Centrifuge', an association of moderate Futurists, 'The Knave of Diamonds', an association of young painters, and 'The Donkey's Tail' a group of Futurist painters who exhibited primitive paintings in Moscow. Others met in an old wooden house in the courtyard of one of the new blocks of flats in Razgulyay Square in Moscow. Here, in an apartment on the top floor, the poet and painter Julian Anisimov was the centre of a circle known as 'Serdarda'. Meanwhile, a sort of school grew up around the Symbolist review *Musaget* under the inspiration of the poet and novelist Andrei Bely, which met often in the studio of the sculptor Krakht in the Presnya district of Moscow to hear lectures by writers or critics on poetic rhythm or kindred subjects. St Petersburg also had its *avant garde* artistic venues. Vyacheslav Ivanov, better known as 'Vyacheslav the Magnificent', a poet and classical scholar, held *soirées* on Wednesday evenings in his seventh-floor apartment called 'The Tower', overlooking the gardens of the Tauride Palace. He had to tear down partitions and extend his apartment to accommodate the numbers who flocked to these events, which rarely became animated until after supper had been served at two o'clock in the morning.

Barbier's illustration of Nijinsky in *Schéhérazade* sums up the spirit of decorative art at this time.

6 Religion Run Riot

Anews item in the Press on 29 June 1914 put all Russia in an uproar: Rasputin, the 'man of God', had been stabbed by a prostitute and lay dangerously ill, on the brink of death. The name Rasputin had been on everybody's lips the whole of that year. No one in the Duma or in the salons, in the towns or in the villages, could talk of anything else. Rasputin, they murmured, and not the Tsar or Tsarina, governed Russia. Mikhail Vladimirovich Rodzianko, President of the Duma, commented, 'The general impression during the winter of 1913–14 was as if the higher society of St Petersburg had suddenly had its eyes opened. Everyone spoke of Rasputin with the greatest apprehension. What had stirred the Duma two years ago had only now reached Court circles.'

Religion mingled with superstition had always been an element of Russian life. The Russian people, from the humblest peasant to the Tsar himself, had always been deeply religious – again with an element of spiritualism tingeing their belief. Ikons hung in every room in every house, keeping watch over family life. In pious households there was a veritable miniature oratory. No important action was taken without their intervention. They were lifted down to watch over the sick and dying, to follow the dead to the cemetery, to officiate at a birth and to serve as witnesses to business deals. They were brought out to bless an engagement and accompanied the bride to the church on her wedding day. Before a member of the family undertook a journey, the whole household sat for a moment in silence together before the ikon, then rose, crossed themselves and kissed the traveller as they wished him or her *bon voyage*.

Russians also crossed themselves on every conceivable occasion – and not only themselves. They made the sign of the cross over those who were dear to them as well as over various articles and food to drive away the powers of evil. Parents crossed their children in their beds at night, wives their husbands as they left for work. Everything blessed by a priest took on a sacred quality and, in a sense, a magical value. Holy water, for example, was frequently given to the sick to drink.

Not only at the times of the great festivals but also on 'name-days', or celebrations of national events, the people flocked to the churches. On the birthday of St Alexander Nevsky, Paléo-logue records, a huge crowd filled the caves and sanctuaries of the monastery which bore his name, and the Cathedral of the Trinity was thick with incense as worshippers swarmed round

the shrine of St Alexander. The Ambassador was particularly struck by one peasant who seemed to him to typify the religious feeling of the whole people: '. . . an old man with snow-white hair and beard, swarthy complexion, broad and deeply wrinkled forehead, melancholy, luminous and distant eyes – the typical patriarch; standing before an ikon of St Alexander, he was turning his cap in his bony fingers, nor did he stop for a moment except to cross himself fervently while bowing low. He muttered an interminable prayer. . . .'

The quality of the music in the Russian Church must have intensified the emotional appeal of the religion. Paléologue writes:

I know no country except Russia where church music attains such heights of mystery and majesty by vocal polyphony alone. . . . What is so particularly splendid in these works is the deep religious feeling; their appeal is to the mysterious recesses of the soul, and they touch the most secret places of the heart. They express and develop with rare feeling all the lyrical elements enshrined in Christian doctrine. They are successively transports of prayer, sighs of despair, appeals for mercy, cries of distress, screams of fear, the anguished voice of repentance, the fervour of regret, the grief of self-abasement, flickers of hope, outpourings of love, transport of holy ecstasy, the splendour of glory and bliss. At times the magic effects attained a most extraordinary and overwhelming intensity by the sudden intervention of two or three bases whose exceptional registers descended nearly an octave below the normal. At the other end the boys have crystal clear voices which rise so high and with such sweetness and purity that they seem to become sheer spirit, superhuman and seraphic. The heavenly songs which Fra Angelico heard within when he painted his angelic choirs could not have been more ethereal. . . .

Ikons were hung in every house as a constant reminder of the presence of God. This is a thirteenth-century ikon of the Novgorod School. The centre motif depicts St George and the dragon, while the smaller ones show scenes from his martyrdom.

No act of domestic or public life, in fact, went unaccompanied by an act of worship. When this act involved the Tsar himself and his household, it assumed truly magnificent proportions. A typical example was the ceremony of the blessing of the waters which was revived at Epiphany 1911 after a lapse of some years. In point of fact, it had been discontinued after an unfortunate incident in 1905 when a cannon firing the royal salute had been trained in the wrong direction. In 1911, however, nothing marred the brilliance of the occasion. The sky was a pure, clear blue, and the sun shone on the snow-covered ice of the Neva as the slim figure of Nicholas II was greeted on the crimson-carpeted steps of a temporary chapel hung with red velvet by a group of priests in bright-woven vestments. Followed by a procession of Grand Dukes, officers and generals attached to the Court, and the Cossacks of the guard in scarlet tunics, they moved forward between lines of troops drawn up on the quay. The party stopped before a hole cut in the ice of the Neva, and, as a great silver cross was dipped three times in the water, the cannons thundered out the salute, and all the bells of the city burst into song.

The scene was no less magnificent inside the Winter Palace. The corridors and staircases of the Palace were crowded with troops in brilliant uniforms: Cossacks in crimson or sapphire blue; Caucasian officers in long white tunics; members of the Rifle Brigade in magenta shirts and dark green fur-trimmed coats; Hussars in white and gold with scarlet, fur-trimmed dolmans; horse guards in white and gold; infantry officers in orange jackets; and the Court servants in gold-embroidered coats and little round hats with ostrich feathers.

In the inner apartments the ladies of the imperial family were gathered in all their splendour. Meriel Buchanan, standing with other members of the diplomatic corps and their families, watched them enter in glittering procession from the imperial chapel. First came the small figure of the Dowager Empress Marie in a dress of white and silver brocade with a long, sweeping train edged with sable. Diamonds sparkled from her silver diadem, her heavy necklace, a gift from her late husband Alexander III, and from the bodice of her gown. Ropes of pearls hung over her shoulders. The Grand Duchess Marie, who followed her, also wore white and silver. Then came Nicholas's two sisters, Xenia, resplendent in enormous emeralds, and Olga, followed by the Grand Duchess Cyril in cornflower blue velvet with sapphires and diamonds in her necklace and diadem. Next in line were the two 'Montenegrin' Grand Duchesses and then Princess Nicholas of Greece, clad in turquoise blue and gold brocade, and the young Grand Duchess Marina Petrovna in soft rose velvet. The royal procession was brought up by a host of *dames du palais* in olive green, and *demoiselles d'honneur* in ruby velvet. All these dresses were made to a uniform pattern, with close-fitting bodices, cut low off the shoulders and with jewelled buttons. They had full skirts opening over petticoats of stiffly embroidered satin. Long trains fell from the shoulders, and tulle veiling hung from the diadems, always in the same colour as the train and sewn with jewels. The whole effect was of a richness and colour unmatched anywhere else in the world. Let it be

added that the solemnities were followed by superb champagne luncheons where the guests forgot their dignity and tucked into lobster salads and chicken patties, whipped cream and pastry tarts, fruit salad and chocolate ice-cream.

The American Ambassador, George Marye, was also moved by Russian religious ceremonial – despite the fatigue engendered by the constant standing which seemed to be an integral part of a Russian Orthodox service. He was present, together with all the Court dignitaries, ministers, high officials and members of the diplomatic corps, in full dress at the last celebration of the Tsar's birthday in Kazan Cathedral on 19 December 1914. It lasted from eleven in the morning until two in the afternoon and gave Marye ample opportunity to observe the scene.

In looking on them all [he wrote], it was not hard to believe that at no other Court in the world could be found such an array of rich and varied costumes. The services were very impressive, the number of the beautifully garbed clergy, the deep, resonant voices of the cantors who read passages from the scriptures and made the responses, the lofty bursts of sacred music and the setting of it all amid the tall, graceful columns of the cathedral rising to majestic heights

The simple faith of the ordinary Russian. A soldier kisses a priest's cross before departing for the Front.

The gilded crosses and onion towers of the Cathedral of the Annunciation in Moscow were typical of the splendour of Russian churches.

behind the devout faces of the congregation, the objects of art which adorned the walls, and the odour of the incense floating in the air all contributed to impress the imagination and the memory.

The deep religious feeling of the Russian people, coupled with the innate superstitious streak that marked their temperament, could frequently cause them to go to extremes. Mystical communities and strange mystic sects existed throughout the country. The search for the mystical, for a closer association with God, was a phenomenon which could be found at all times and at all levels of Russian society. Russian Court circles and high society in the first quarter of the twentieth century were no exception. In the fashionable salons of St Petersburg lights were turned low, and credulous nobles dabbled in the black arts. A typical example was the 'black salon' held by Countess Ignatiev three times a week, where old ladies, generals and members of the Church sought admittance to the magic world of the spirits. Once, when Count Ignatiev had been alive, it had been an influential political hearth, and its reputation as a hotbed of reaction and the home of autocracy and theocracy still remained. Promotions in the ecclesiastical hierarchy, nominations to the Holy Synod, the most serious questions of dogma, discipline and Church liturgy were all discussed there. But of equal, if not superior, interest to its devotees were the whispered confidences exchanged of signs received and manifestations witnessed, of the new 'holy men' discovered.

Interest in the cult of mysticism did not stop at the nobility. It extended to the Court itself. One faction was particularly susceptible. This was centred around the two Montenegrin princesses, sisters who had married two Russian Grand Dukes, uncles of the Tsar. The Grand Duchess Militsa was the wife of Peter Nikolaenich; her sister Anastasia was married to his brother the Grand Duke Nicholas. They headed the mystical group in St Petersburg and were the principal patrons of the variety of mystics whom, at one time or another, it became fashionable to patronize.

There was, for example, one Mitia Koliaba, who was brought to St Petersburg in 1901. Nothing about Mitia suggested a man of God. He was deaf, dumb, half-blind, bandy-legged and deformed, both mentally and physically. In place of arms, he had two stumps, and these he waved to accompany the guttural cries, stammering, grunts, roars and squeals which served to express his limited ideas. It was when this sad individual went into a fit which was diagnosed as a trance at the Optina-Pustyn monastery near Kozielsk where he was receiving charity, that it was realized that he was a vehicle for divine communication. The nature of this communication was conveyed to a monk at the monastery by St Nicholas in a vision, and everyone was astounded by the breadth of knowledge of past, present and future that the noises of the half-wit concealed. He became an authority on foretelling the future and was finally brought to St Petersburg in this capacity to become the oracle for the fashionable set.

He had to share Court acclaim with another mystic of a quite different sort, who was practising in the city at the same time. This was a Frenchman, Philippe Nazier-Vachod, a professional soul-doctor who had twice been prosecuted in his native land for practising medicine without a licence. He was a mild little man with gentle manners, a high forehead and thick dark hair, but his whole strength was concentrated in his eyes. Half-hidden by heavy eyelids, they were blue, limpid, fascinating and penetrating, at the same time full of sympathy and magnetism. Witnesses report that kindness, pity and unselfishness emanated from his mere presence, and a gentle balm flowed from his slightest movement. From humble beginnings, his powers of soothing and strengthening those around him brought him from a butcher's shop in France via a Parisian society practice to a villa near the Tsar's home in Tsarskoe Selo.

In fact, the patronage which brought Philippe to Russia came from no less exalted a source than the Tsar and Tsarina. They had been introduced to him by the Grand Duchess Militsa when they visited Paris in 1900 and were so impressed that they invited him to Russia and prepared a house for him at Tsarskoe. Once he was there, rumour said that Philippe spent one or two evenings a week with the imperial couple, carrying out experiments in hypnotism, prophecy, incarnation and necromancy. It was even suggested that the Tsar received messages from his father, Alexander III, during these sessions.

It would appear, indeed, that the Tsar and certainly the Tsarina were not untouched by the current interest in mysticism. At the time when Philippe entered their lives, their major concern was providing the nation with an heir. Alexandra had to date presented her husband with four daughters. She was desperate for a boy. In 1902, Philippe diagnosed a new pregnancy and furthermore was able to prophesy that the child in her womb was male. Unfortunately for his reputation, no less than for Russia, his diagnoses were incorrect (or if they were accurate, the Tsarina had a miscarriage). No child was born. Philippe's career rapidly came to an end, though not before he had made the dramatic pronouncement, 'You will some day have another friend like me who will speak to you of God.'

Nicholas and Alexandra, fearing that they had incurred the wrath of God, who was therefore preventing them from giving birth to a son, hastened to propitiate him by intervening in 1903 to bring about the canonization of a somewhat dubious saint, Seraphim, a pious old man of Sarov. In 1904 the wished-for boy was born. Alexandra did not fail to connect the two events.

In 1903, even before the Tsarevich was born, rumours of the advent of a new prophet in the land were already running through St Petersburg: a peasant from the village of Pokrovskoie in the province of Tobolsk, whose name was Gregory Rasputin. On 29 December 1903, when Rasputin first appeared at the Religious Academy of St Petersburg, a monk there by the name

Rasputin the peasant, seen here with his children at Pokrovskoie.

148

of Illiodor described him as a stocky peasant of middle height, with ragged, dirty hair falling over his shoulders, a tangled beard and steely grey eyes, deep-set under bushy eyebrows, and a strong body odour. He appeared as a man who had been a great sinner and was now a great penitent, who drew extraordinary power from the experiences he had undergone. It should be noted that the name he had adopted, 'Rasputin', has sometimes been interpreted to mean 'the dissolute' – and he had, in fact, shocked even his native village by his sexual insolence.

Be that as it may, his reputation for holiness grew daily – though at Tsarytsin he was said to have deflowered a nun he had undertaken to exorcise; though at Kazan he was reported to have emerged from a drinking den thrashing a naked prostitute with his belt; though at Tobolsk he seduced the wife of a well-established engineer, a very pious woman who introduced him to the refined joys of society women. His opportunities to enjoy them were to increase. It was not just the ordinary people who knelt down in the streets as he passed, kissing his hands, touching the hem of his robe, calling out: 'Our Christ, Our Saviour, pray for us poor sinners!' In 1905 the Archimandrite Theophanes, Rector of the Theological College at St Petersburg, the Tsarina's confessor, summoned him and introduced him into the very influential circle of which the Montenegrin Grand Duchesses formed part. Enveloped in mysticism as they were, they were fascinated by Rasputin, more particularly after he had effected a miraculous cure of Grand Duke Nicholas's dog. His powers over humans were also attested; he had cured the son of his friend Aron Simanovich, a Jewish jeweller, of St Vitus' Dance.

But even greater honours were in store. On 1 November 1905, on the recommendation of Militsa and Anastasia, Rasputin was called to the Palace. That evening, Tsar Nicholas wrote in his diary: 'We have got to know a man of God – Gregory – from the Tobolsk province.' Before proceeding further, however, they consulted Theophanes, who reassured them:

Gregory Efimovich is a peasant, a man of the people. Your Majesties will do well to hear him, for it is the voice of the Russian soil which speaks through him. . . . I know his sins, which are numberless and most of them heinous. But there dwells in him so deep a passion of repentance and so implicit a trust in divine pity that I would all but guarantee his eternal salvation. Every time he repents he is as pure as the child washed in the waters of baptism. Manifestly God has called him to be one of His chosen.

With the blessings of the Archimandrite, there was no longer anything to prevent Nicholas and Alexandra from pursuing their acquaintance with Rasputin. On the other hand, there was everything to make it desirable in their eyes. Apart from the deep religion and interest in mysticism which they both possessed, there was the attraction of actual contact with the Russian peasantry. Rasputin, they had been told, spoke with the voice of the Russian soil, and both Tsar and Tsarina were very conscious of their inability to learn what were the real thoughts of the masses of their people. Rasputin seemed to them the very incarnation of this, particularly as he made a point of treating them with bold and disingenuous familiarity right from the start. Accustomed as they were to flattery and adulation, they found his 'stable language', 'incredible insolence' and disgusting table-manners refreshing. He was known to plunge his hands into his favourite fish soup at the most distinguished tables.

Other people did not find his conduct so attractive or consider it genuine. Count Kokovstov, Chairman of the Council of Ministers, described him as

a typical Siberian tramp, a clever man who had trained himself for the role of a simpleton and a madman and who played his part according to a set formula. He did not believe in his tricks himself but had trained himself to certain mannerisms of conduct in order to deceive those who sincerely believed in all his oddities. Others, of course, merely pretended to admire him, hoping to obtain privileges through him which could not be obtained in any other way.

However, feminine reaction, as illustrated by a certain 'Countess B——' whom the French Ambassador Paléologue quotes, was rather different. Physically, she agreed, she found him disgusting, and was repelled by his dirty hands, black nails and unkempt beard. But yet, she said, 'he has extraordinary verve and imagination. At times he is actually eloquent. He has a gift for metaphor and a deep sense of mystery. . . . He is familiar, mocking, violent, merry, ridiculous and poetical by turns. And with all this not a trace of pose! On the contrary, the most unexampled effrontery and the most staggering cynicism.'

However, the over-riding reason which caused Nicholas and Alexandra to deepen their contact with Rasputin was their faith in his power to heal their son. Medicine was powerless to aid them in their battle for his life against the dread disease haemophilia. In the face of man's impotence, they turned more and

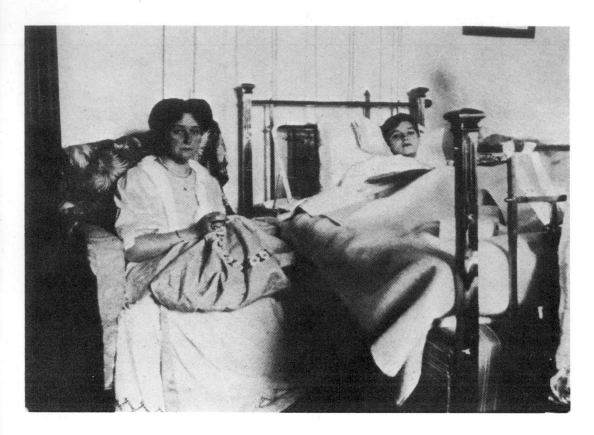

more to God – or to the man whom they believed to be God's representative on earth.

Rasputin did indeed prove to have some mystical curative powers as far as young Alexis was concerned. A typical incident occurred at Spala (an ancient hunting-seat of the kings of Poland) in 1912. While messing about in a boat, Alexis stretched out his leg at the wrong moment, hit it on the side of the boat and bruised it. An internal haemorrhage was set up in the groin. The child was in agony, and fears for his life grew as his condition deteriorated daily. The doctors in attendance could do nothing to arrest the bleeding, and specialists were summoned from St Petersburg. But the invalid's temperature continued to rise, and prayers for his recovery were said twice daily in a tent erected in the park with a small portable altar. In his bedroom the child lay white-faced and wasted, wailing with the intensity of the pain, which nothing could soothe. For the first time, medical bulletins were issued warning the country that the life of their heir was in danger. The Tsarina sat helplessly by the bed of her son. In desperation, she telegraphed to Rasputin, asking him to pray for Alexis. The same evening, a reply arrived: 'God has seen your tears and heard your prayers. Grieve no more! Your son will live. Don't let the doctors worry him.' The Tsarevich's recovery is said to date from the following morning.

Was it surprising then that the Tsarina placed whole-hearted faith in Rasputin? He must surely be the man of God. His prayers had snatched Alexis from the mouth of death. It seemed to her that the survival of the heir depended entirely on Rasputin. And on the survival of the heir depended the survival of the dynasty and the future of Russia. As the months passed, her dependence on him increased.

In the country, on the other hand, Rasputin was rapidly falling into disrepute. His theological supporters gradually withdrew. First the Archimandrite Theophanes, then Hermogen, Bishop of Savator and the monk Illiodor repudiated him, the latter following a particularly unsavoury episode. In an unguarded moment, Rasputin boastfully showed Illiodor a collection of letters he claimed that the Tsarina had written him. They included such phrases as 'My head bows; I feel your hand. . . .' Illiodor, so the story goes, pocketed a couple of these letters while Rasputin was out of the room and, after his break with Rasputin, threatened to publish them. Mimeographed copies were circulated, and a Press campaign against Rasputin was initiated. The question was even raised in the Duma.

An early Rasputin scandal had already been in circulation in 1909 when the under-governess of the imperial children had spread rumours that Rasputin was a frequent visitor to the imperial nurseries. He regularly bathed the young Grand Duchesses, Mademoiselle Tutchev said, and then sat on their beds talking to them. Mademoiselle Tutchev was dismissed, but the talk she had engendered continued. During 1911 and 1912 the Press campaign against Rasputin intensified. Count Kokovtsov reported that even the Dowager Empress was deeply disturbed. 'My poor daughter-in-law', she said to him, 'does not perceive that she is ruining both the dynasty and herself. She sincerely believes in the holiness of an adventurer, and we are powerless to ward off the misfortune which is sure to come.' Alexandra's sister, the Grand Duchess Elizabeth, widow of the Grand Duke Serge, also tried to convince her that Rasputin was a charlatan – to no avail. The isolation of the imperial couple from their immediate family only increased.

Rasputin's apartment in St Petersburg, at 64, Govokhovaia Street, was a hive of dubious activity. Despite the aura of 'middle class solidity' that Prince Felix Youssoupov discerned there, other witnesses describe scenes of hysteria and debauchery, as gatherings of adoring women wishing to consult the man of God sat on high-backed chairs around the massive oak dining-room table, waiting. . . . There was nothing for their eyes to rest upon except a bulky dresser full of crockery against one wall, a few badly painted pictures, a bronze chandelier with glass shades. Behind a closed door was the small, simply furnished bedroom. A narrow bed covered with a red fox bedspread (a gift from Anna Vrubova) stood against the wall in one corner close to a big painted chest. On the walls were ikons with a lamp burning in front of them, portraits of Nicholas and Alexandra, and some crude engravings of biblical scenes.

Within these walls came and went Rasputin's close associates, including a Dr Badmaiev, a medical practitioner with no recognized qualifications but who prospered on his reputation for having brought all sorts of medicinal herbs and magical remedies back from a visit to Mongolia. He had no hesitation in treating the most obscure ailments but had a preference for nervous diseases, mental illness and the intricacies of female physiology. He did a dangerous trade in narcotics, stupefactives, anaesthetics and aphrodisiacs under such names as 'Elixir du Thibet', 'Poudre de Nirvritti', 'Fleur d'Asokas', and 'Essence de Lotus Noir'. Nicholas and Alexandra were said to have called Dr Badmaiev in to attend Alexis in times of dire emergency.

Another intimate of Rasputin's was a certain Prince Andronnikov, a political schemer of the first order. Carrying his bulging, bright yellow attaché case, he was often to be seen entering Rasputin's chambers at a brisk pace and just as quickly bustling out again. For Andronnikov was always in a hurry and perpetually busy. He knew everyone, but, more important, he knew everything, even the most secret decisions of the Tsar, hours before they became public (it was said that his information was based on a long-standing friendship with the Tsar's groom). He too held a salon at his home, to which officers, officials and churchmen flocked in the hope of learning of new developments or of presenting by this devious means their requests to the Court for appointments or honours.

Another *habitué* of the apartment was a very sharp character, Manasevich-Maniulov, a man who dressed with elegance in

tight-fitting black coat, with slicked-down hair, and whom Paléologue describes as an 'agent provocateur, spy, sharper, swindler, cheat, forger and rake in one'. Rumour linked his name with Okhrana (secret police) activities, the instigation of strikes among the workers, and pogroms against his Jewish co-religionists. He and Rasputin were closely linked in many dubious dealings, and entry to the inner sanctum was rarely denied him by Rasputin's secretary, the fashionable Court jeweller Aron Simanovich.

Such were Rasputin's friends. But other callers at the apartment were said to be involved with the 'man of God' in business dealings, speculations and investment. One of these was the financier Ignati Porfirievich Manus, noted for his manipulation of the St Petersburg Stock Exchange. Risen from poor circumstances by dubious means to a position of some influence in banking circles, he was known as 'the yellow man'. His was the money behind the politically important St Petersburg Burdukov salon. Burdukov was the Imperial Master of the Horse; he was attached to the Ministry of the Interior, and he was also on terms of some intimacy with two of the Emperor's *aides-de-camp*. Herein lay his strength. In possession of advance political information, he was able to purvey it to the most profitable buyer and

The incongruous spectacle of the wild-eyed, dishevelled Rasputin surrounded by adoring, well-dressed society women at a tea party in his apartment.

equally to convey requests and 'suggestions' to the Court when it seemed desirable.

Mingling with these men on the stairs leading to the apartment were a host of ordinary police, secret police and special agents, some of them disguised as servants. Their task was to record every movement Rasputin made, when he went out, where he went, whom he met, when he came back, as well as to note down the names of everyone who entered the apartment. According to Fülöp-Miller, a biographer of Rasputin, the contents of these notebooks read somewhat as follows:

14 October : Rasputin came home drunk at 1 a.m., insulted the *concierge*'s wife and reproached her with taking a bribe of twenty-five roubles from a minister. Then he remarked: 'He tried to bury me, but now I will bury him.'

6 November : Rasputin was at Popermann, the merchant from Samara's flat, and came back drunk five hours later, kissing Popermann when he said good-bye. As he went up to his flat, he inquired if there were any visitors for him. On hearing that there were two ladies, he asked: 'Are they pretty? Very pretty? That's good. I need pretty ones.' About seven o'clock he left the house and gave the *concierge*'s wife ten roubles; he seemed to be dead with sleep.

14 November : Rasputin came home at 5 a.m., blind drunk.

3 December : Rasputin came home drunk at 3 a.m.

8 January : Rasputin came home from a visit to Nordmann, the Secretary of the Chancellery of the Order, about 3 a.m. accompanied by three ladies. The ladies stayed with him for two hours.

14 January : Rasputin came home at 7 a.m.; he was dead drunk. He had Ossipenko and an unknown man with him. He smashed a pane of glass in the house door; apparently he had had one fall already, for his nose was swollen. . . .

– and so on.

From the notes it would seem that his sexual exploits continued, and if they did not lead into the imperial Court (as was at times scurrilously suggested), they certainly reached some of the leading St Petersburg salons. Society ladies considered it a privilege to submit their bodies to his desires. They sought the humiliation and the novel sensation thus involved and were happy to accept Rasputin's promise that physical contact with himself was a purification.

Rasputin's message was simple:

It is by repentance alone that we can win our salvation. We must therefore sin in order to have an opportunity for repentance. So when God places temptation in our way, it is our duty to yield, so we may secure the necessary condition precedent to a salutary penitence. Besides, was not the first word of life and truth which Christ uttered to mankind 'Repent'? But how can we repent if we have not sinned?

Rasputin made no secret of his love of wine and women. At his first meeting with Mossolov, he was, on his own admission, '... boozed, dead drunk. ... Does it upset you? I understand. ... Don't take any notice. ... One day, when there's more time, we'll talk more seriously. ... But not now. Here's to your health!'

'We had several glasses together', [Mossolov writes]. 'You must come over to see me one day ... everybody comes to see me ... the Ministers ... and Vitia [Witte] too ... only you and your old man [Count Fredericks] make a fuss about it. That's why Mamma [the Empress] doesn't like you any longer.'
'I suppose this intrigue was your little scheme?' [Mossolov was referring to an incident whereby he had lost the Empress's confidence.]
'What of that? Of course it was! Love me, and Mamma will love you.'
'There now, you're the sort I like. You don't bear ill-will. Anybody who can lift it can't have any guile in him. I don't mind a bottle now and then myself.'
'When he left', [Mossolov comments] 'he ruined my overcoat in the hall.' [And, as a *coup de grâce*.] 'Next day I found myself once more in the Empress's good graces.'

Nor was any concealment possible in relation to Rasputin's evenings of debauchery in the nightspots of St Petersburg and Moscow. A lady called Elena Dianumova is reported (again by Fülöp-Miller) as describing one such episode which began to warm up when the party reached Moscow's Yar restaurant. It contains all the ingredients of the Rasputin story, including the secret police, fear and antagonism.

... Rasputin was at once recognized, and the proprietor, fearing a scandal such as had already occurred there, immediately communicated with the Prefect, who despatched two officials to the restaurant. They arrived in the shortest possible time, came to our room and asked to be allowed to remain, on the ground that they had to protect Rasputin against possible attacks; soon afterwards several police officers in plain clothes appeared with the same object. ...

Meanwhile the gipsy choir, with the famous singer Nastia Polakova, had come on the stage; Rasputin began to feel happy and ordered fruit, coffee, cakes and champagne.

It was incredible how much Rasputin could drink. Anybody else would rapidly have fallen down insensible, but with him the only signs were that his eyes grew brighter, his face paler and his wrinkles deeper.

'Now then,' he shouted suddenly, 'begin to sing, children.' Behind the screen which cut off our room two guitars began to twang, and the voices of the gipsy girls were heard; Rasputin sat in silence and listened with bowed head. 'Nastia,' he declared, at the end, 'you sing so beautifully that it grips the heart.'

Then all at once he jumped up and joined in the singing in his full, clear voice. 'And now, Nastia,' he called, 'we'll drink a glass. I love gipsy songs, and when I hear them, my heart exults with joy.'

'Now sing my favourite song, the "*Troika*",' cried Rasputin, jumping up. He was pale and stood before us with half-shut eyes; with his hair falling over his forehead, he began to beat time with his hands: I go, I go to her, to my love.

His voice was full of fire and passion, and its tones stamped themselves deeply on my memory. What elemental strength lay hidden in this man!

The party later moved on to the Strelna, where a large reserved room was assigned to them. Champagne flowed freely.

Rasputin was now in his element: while a Russian dance was being played, he whirled wildly and impetuously through the room, his black hair and his great beard flying from one side to the other. His feet, in their heavy top-boots, moved with amazing lightness, and it seemed as if the wine had multiplied his powers. From time to time he burst into wild cries, seized one of the gipsies and danced with her. . . .

Excursions like these might, at a pinch, have been tolerated. Rasputin's dominance over the Tsarina might have been endured. His custom of assisting his friends or supplicants to office or privilege by presenting them with a personal note of commendation to an important person might have been suffered – though these sheets of paper proliferated. Paléologue vividly describes the

. . . large, uneven, heavy and uneducated handwriting, a jumble of jerks, stabs and contortions. The letters were so clumsy and misshapen that it was exceedingly difficult to make them out. But, taken as a whole, the sheet was as expressive as an etching; one could feel the trembling of the hand as it traced each word, and before one's eyes rose the vision of a being endowed with imagination and audacity, a thing of impulses and sensuality. The signature was always easy to read: Rasputin.

Mossolov actually received one such note. It was handed to him by a young lady who invaded his office one day in official visiting hours, wearing a low-cut dress. He disliked her at sight. 'My dear chap. Fix it up for her. She is all right. Rasputin', ran the note. It transpired that the visitor wanted to become a *prima donna* at the Imperial Opera Company in St Petersburg. Mossolov had no difficulty in resisting her attractions and no compunction in explaining to her that he could not help her.

What was inadmissible was the influence over political affairs that Rasputin came to wield. That the Tsar took Rasputin's advice on the appointment of ministers was already an acknowledged fact. In the spring of 1911, for example, Rasputin had accompanied the Foreign Minister, Sergei Dimitrievich Sazonov, to Nizhny Novgorod on imperial instructions to interview one Alexei Nicolaevich Khostov to see if he would make a suitable Minister of the Interior.

It gradually became apparent, however, that not only was Rasputin's advice sought but also that officials and ministers who spoke out against Rasputin were humiliated, if not dismissed. Those who supported him prospered. This was not by any means always to the country's advantage. Feelings against him ran so high that it was no surprise when on 29 June 1914, it was learned that a serious attempt had been made on his life. He had just embarked on a return visit to his native Pokrovskoie when he was stabbed in the stomach by a prostitute whose lover he had been. To the shout, 'I've killed the Antichrist!' she drove the knife deeply into his entrails. Alexandra, in enforced inactivity cruising the Finnish fjords, was distraught. She is said to have telegraphed to Tobolsk every day. Rasputin, as if to prove his supernatural powers, miraculously recovered.

7 The Imperial Family

In March 1913 Russia celebrated the tercentenary of the Romanov dynasty. In 1613 Mikhail Feodorovich Romanov had been elected to rule over the vast country; 300 years later the reigning monarch was Nicholas II. Much had changed over that period. Some would have said that the introduction of the Duma, the first elected government Russia had ever known, after the internal troubles of 1905, had more radically altered the status of the Tsar–autocrat than any other event in those 300 years. Nicholas, however, still saw himself as a complete Tsar–autocrat, ruling over a subservient population – a direct descendant of his illustrious predecessors.

It was not surprising, therefore, to find a critical attitude towards the tercentenary proceedings being taken by those Russians pledged to a more liberal, even parliamentary, form of government. One such was Count Kokovtsov, Chairman of the Council of Ministers at the time, who regretfully commented that, 'the concepts of state and government were to be pushed into the background, and the personality of the Tsar was to dominate the scene. The current attitude seemed to suggest that the government was a barrier between the people and their Tsar, whom they regarded with blind devotion as anointed by God.' Both the ministers and the Duma, he suggested, thought that the sovereign should recognize that conditions had changed since the day the Romanovs became Tsars of Moscow and lords of the Russian domain. Mikhail Vladimirovich Rodzianko, President of the Duma, sounded a different warning. 'If the Romanov jubilee was intended to be a national rejoicing', he wrote, 'it should not be overlooked that in 1613 it was an assembly of the people and not a group of officials that elected Mikhail Feodorovich Romanov Tsar of Russia.'

Expressions of fealty on the occasion of the tercentenary reached the imperial family from all corners of the Empire. The Postal Department issued commemorative stamps portraying Peter the Great, Catherine II, Alexander II, Alexander III and Nicholas II. But Kokovtsov saw only lack of enthusiasm and hollow curiosity in the crowds thronging the gaily decorated streets of St Petersburg on 6 March when a solemn *Te Deum* was sung in the city's Kazan Cathedral. The church was filled to capacity and beyond, when the Patriarch Antiochus, resplendent in a great bejewelled mitre, conducted the service himself in the presence of the Tsar and Tsarina. Never had the singing been so beautiful. Never had the glory of the Cathedral shown

to greater advantage and sparkled with such an array of jewel-like colours: the silver ikonostasis, the golden ikons, the green, purple and crimson vestments of the priests, the varied brilliant uniforms of the military and diplomatic members of the congregation, the flickering lights of the hundreds of candles, and the 103 tattered flags, emblazoned with the imperial eagles of Napoleon's *Grande Armée*, which hung between the fifty-six granite Corinthian columns, with their bronze bases and capitals. It was noticed that both the Tsar and his son were looking upwards for some time during the ceremony. Nicholas later explained that two doves had hovered over their heads for several minutes. He interpreted this as a sign that God's blessing still reigned over the House of Romanov. Only one important incident marred the solemnity of the occasion. With a certain amount of difficulty, Rodzianko had exchanged the rather inferior block of seats in the Cathedral reserved for members of the Duma for the superior block reserved for the Senate. What was his astonishment, therefore, to find on entering that Rasputin, the Empress's favourite, was comfortably ensconced in one of them – and dressed to kill at that. The 'man of God' wore a magnificent tunic of crimson silk, patent leather top-boots, black cloth full trousers and a peasant's overcoat. To crown it all, a pectoral cross on a finely wrought gold chain hung round his neck. In an absolute fury Rodzianko seized Rasputin by the scruff of his neck and forcibly ejected him.

In the evening there was a gala performance at the Maryinsky Theatre. Mathilde Kschessinska came out of mourning for her mother to dance the mazurka from the second act of the opera *La Vie pour le Tsar*. But the sensation of the performance was undoubtedly the unprecedented appearance of the first Romanov Tsar, Mikhail Feodorovich, portrayed by Sobinov (standing in for Chaliapin who had been taken ill at the last moment). For the first time for many years, the Tsarina Alexandra accompanied her husband to the ballet, wearing a white velvet gown, its bodice embellished by the pale blue ribbon of St Andrew and ablaze with diamonds. She wore a turquoise and diamond tiara and carried a white ostrich feather fan. The imperial couple watched the performance from gold-backed armchairs in the big centre loge, while all four of the royal boxes near to the stage were filled with members of the imperial family, and all three tiers of boxes glittered with jewels and tiaras. The stalls below were entirely filled with the scarlet uniforms of the Court officials who looked, to quote Meriel Buchanan, like 'a field of poppies' when they rose to greet their Tsar.

Festivities continued on 7 March, when an enormous ball was held in the Assembly Hall of the Nobles, attended by all available members of the imperial family as well as hundreds of other guests. The Tsar opened the ball with his wife, who wore a sweeping white and silver gown with a magnificent diamond tiara on her fair hair and cascades of diamonds rippling over her shoulders. At the head of a procession of Grand Dukes, they executed a solemn polonaise to the music of Chopin, moving slowly round the hall, changing partners at the end of each round. Their eldest daughter, Olga, was with them that evening, making one of her earliest public appearances. Everyone commented on her charm, as, dressed in a simple pale pink chiffon gown, her fair hair shining like burnished gold, blue eyes sparkling, she danced every dance with obvious enjoyment. Among the interested onlookers speculation was rife as to which Grand Duke she would eventually marry. . . .

The days that ensued were filled for the imperial couple with the reception of delegations from all over the Empire, when the women appeared in the picturesque costumes of their locality. Alexandra also wore Russian national dress and looked truly regal in richly flowing robes and a long veiled high *kokochnik* (head-dress). The Grand Duchesses appeared on these occasions simply but beautifully turned out, their sole adornment being the Order of Catherine the Great, a red ribbon with blazing diamond stars, worn over white dresses.

The celebrations included a *levée* at the Winter Palace attended by all the members of the Duma. It was on this occasion that Rodzianko formally presented to Nicholas, on behalf of his colleagues, a beautiful ikon of rare antiquity and a white linen tapestry, twenty yards long, depicting the first Tsar welcoming his father on his arrival in Moscow. Rodzianko's was the only speech made that evening – a fact which he considered significant.

Then, in May, the imperial family embarked on a grand tour of all the major Russian towns connected with the Romanov dynasty. Leaving Tsarskoe Selo on 28 May, they went via Moscow to Vladimir, Bogolioubov and Nizhny Novgorod. Here they took to the water and sailed on a river-boat down the Volga. But, though landing-stages, gaily decorated and crowded with peasants, marked out their route, the waiting groups were not to be rewarded for their patience. There was a biting cold wind,

and the Tsar did not emerge once, nor did the steamer stop until it reached Kostromo where the first Romanov Tsar had been offered the crown at the Ipatiev Convent. Here they spent the night and, incidentally, again according to Kokovtsov, encountered some real enthusiasm for the tour and also a spell of warm weather. Here, too, they met Rasputin, who appeared, no one knew from where, in one of the churches. Then the party continued by water to Jaroslav where they boarded the imperial train, equipped with every conceivable luxury, and travelled onwards to Pereislavl and Rostov Veliki. Wherever they went, they were greeted by cheering crowds. Devoted subjects waded waist-high into the water to be nearer to the Tsar's boat and perhaps to catch a glimpse of him. In the towns, workmen fell to the ground to kiss his shadow as he passed. At the Kostromo Convent, ikons were presented and loyal speeches made.

It was, in truth, a triumphal procession. Yet there was an aura of disappointment accompanying the celebrations. Hopes regarding a general amnesty of political prisoners and other concessions to be granted by the Tsar in honour of the anniversary were incompletely fulfilled, and Kokovtsov could comment, 'There was brilliance and a motley throng but complete unawareness of the dangers which beset Russia both at home and abroad.'

Moscow celebrated the centenary with equal pomp, rejoicing and expressions of loyalty. The Tsar left his car a little way from the Kremlin and passed through the gates of the city on foot, preceded by chanting priests carrying censers and holy images. Alexandra and their son followed close behind him in an open car. According to Kokovtsov, the crowd which preceded them and which thronged the Krasnaia Ploshchad was smaller than usual. He also noted that, at some points in the ceremonial, the Tsarevich was carried along in the arms of an enormous Cossack, exciting expressions of sympathy from the crowd as the procession paused before the Minin and Pozhaisky monument. How sad, the people murmured, to see the heir to the Romanov throne so weak, so sickly and so helpless. Spent with these exertions, triumphant after so many expressions of the love and devotion of his country and his people, the Tsar then retired to spend a short time in the autumn holidaying with his family in Livadia.

It was at times like these that he was at his happiest. He hated St Petersburg: 'You are probably envious of me', he said to

Nicholas and Alexandra in traditional Russian costume during the tercentenary celebrations. Their major tours of the country at this time, intended to express solidarity with the Russian people, were on the whole a failure.

и Государыня Императрица, Великія Княжны Ольга и
Татіана Николаевны
въ прогулкѣ въ Финляндскихъ шхерахъ.

Kokovtsov on one occasion when he was leaving it for the country, 'but I am not envious of you. I am only sorry for you who have to remain in this bog.' Another time, when away from the city, he told Monsieur Paléologue, 'We feel these Petrograd miasmas even here, twenty-two versts away. And it isn't from the poor quarters but the drawing-rooms that the worst smells come!' St Petersburg to Nicholas meant above all the business of governing his vast and unruly country. It was a mission for which he was eminently unsuited. He was a shy, somewhat retiring man, who disliked any form of unpleasantness. He shied from the disagreeable task of dismissing his own ministers. A minister would be cordially and affably received by the Tsar one day – to discover a written request for his resignation on his desk the next. Unfortunately, such dismissals were frequent occurrences. Nicholas listened to any advice he was tendered and was easily swayed by it. The result was that his policy followed a wavering and unsteady course, not entirely to the advantage of the nation. It is extraordinary to find that, with a temperament such as this, Nicholas (strongly supported by Alexandra) held firmly to the tradition of the Tsar as an autocrat, exercising absolute power. To him, it was a sacred trust, handed on to him by his father. It was his bounden duty to pass it on, in his turn, to his son, the little Tsarevich Alexis.

A family man *par excellence*, his most contented moments were spent with his son in the simplicity of family life. As for his wife, the Tsarina Alexandra, she too disliked St Petersburg; it reminded her of earlier, happier times. 'I was so happy then,' she told her friend Anna Vrubova, 'so well and strong. Now I am a wreck.' Moreover, she found the gaiety and superficiality of high society and the formality of state occasions there intolerable and unendurable. Both at the gala ballet performance and at the tercentenary ball she was observed to be struggling manfully against her nerves. At both functions, she had to withdraw in the face of rapidly mounting hysteria and faintness. 'The Empress', says Foreign Minister Sazonov, 'displayed nothing but weariness as she always did on such occasions.' Since 1905, in fact, she had virtually withdrawn from all public functions.

After that year which marked Russia's ignominious defeat in the war with Japan and the country's violent internal disturbances which seriously threatened the Tsar's sovereignty, it had seemed inappropriate to both Tsar and Tsarina to resume their brilliant Court life. They no longer lived in the magnificent

The Tsar was at his happiest when living a simple life as father of his family.

ABOVE The Tsar and one of his daughters out rowing, while the Tsarina and another daughter relax in the stern.

BELOW A delightful picture of the Tsarevich with Tatiana, the most beautiful of the Grand Duchesses, flanked by the Tsar and Prince Nikita.

169

Winter Palace in St Petersburg. They had never liked its vast gloominess and in any case felt that the garden there was not large enough for their children. Instead, their winters were spent in Tsarskoe Selo, and their summers mainly in Peterhof or Livadia. Since January 1903 there had been no great royal ball at the Winter Palace, which had once glittered two or three times every season with a display of brilliant colour.

Sir George Buchanan, British Ambassador to St Petersburg between 1910–18, remembered only one occasion during the whole period of his ministry when the doors of the Winter Palace were opened for anything beyond the formal New Year reception and the ceremony of the Blessing of the Waters at Epiphany. This was in the winter of 1913–14 when the heads of missions and leading members of Russian society were invited to a performance of *Parsifal* in the private theatre in the Hermitage, built for Catherine the Great. His comment did not match the momentous nature of the event: 'The dinner, however, that was served in the Winter Palace during one of the *entr'actes* hardly came up to one's expectations after all that one heard of the splendours of such entertainments in the past. Neither from a spectacular nor from a gastronomic standpoint could it compare with a State Banquet at Buckingham Palace.'

Some erstwhile guests did still remember the balls when thousands of palm trees and exotic plants were brought in from the Crimea, and masses of roses, tulips and lilacs imported from the Tsarskoe Selo hot-houses, when the white, silver and gold uniforms of the Chevalier Guards lined the staircase and corridors; they recalled the crimson and blue *cherkeskas* of the Cossack Life Guards, the scarlet of the Negro footmen, the senior Court ladies in olive green, the maids-of-honour in ruby-red velvet. . . .

At one time, Nicholas had the idea of abolishing all the modern uniforms of the Court dignitaries and replacing them by copies of the costumes of the sixteenth-century boyars. An artist had been employed to work out models, but it had been found that the boyar costumes, with all their furs and jewels, were too costly, and the scheme was dropped. Nevertheless, Nicholas himself when at home always wore a sort of Russian peasant blouse – seen by some as a further symptom of his intense love of all things Russian.

The simplicity of his dress was, however, symptomatic. The day of the palace balls was past. Now, while society continued its merry scandalous winter whirl in St Petersburg, the imperial

The Peterhof, with the ornamental fountains playing in the foreground.

family lived in Tsarskoe Selo in almost cloistral simplicity. Their idyll there was protected by a host of faithful servants whose task it was to ensure that they never became aware of the illusory nature of their hot-house happiness. Gradually their isolation from the Court, let alone from the ordinary people, had become almost complete. Even Sazonov, most tolerant of Foreign Ministers, bemoaned the fact. 'It is pitiable,' he wrote, 'little by little, a vacuum has formed round the imperial couple; none can approach them; with the exception of the official relations between the Emperor and his ministers, no voice from

The Alexander Palace
at Tsarskoe Selo,
which Nicholas and
Alexandra preferred
to the larger Great
Palace.

the outside world ever penetrates to the Palace.' An anonymous
Princess R—— described the situation to the French Ambassador Paléologue in even stronger terms:

Isn't it grievous to think that the masters of Russia live in such
an atmosphere. It's as if they lived in rooms which are never aired.
Just think, no one – I mean it, no one – ever sees them alone or lunches
with them or goes for a walk with them, or dines with them or spends
an evening with them . . . not a soul except Anna Vrubova. When
I remember what my parents told me of the Courts of Alexander II
and Alexander III, it makes me want to cry. No doubt they had their
intrigues, feuds, favoritism and even scandals, as all Courts have.
But at any rate there was some life about them. The monarchs were
approachable; you could talk quite freely with them so that they
learned a good deal. In turn you got to know – and like – them. But
now – what a contrast, what a lapse! . . .

If their contact with high society was non-existent, even their
relationship with some members of the imperial family had
became strained over the years. Alexandra had resented her
mother-in-law, the Dowager Empress Marie, from the start.
She was particularly distressed by the fact that in the months
following his coronation, Nicholas had depended heavily on his
mother for advice on the conduct of foreign affairs and the general

policy of the country. She had likewise resented the attempts of Nicholas's aunt Marie Pavlovna to help her adapt to the ways of Russian society in the early days after her arrival there. By 1914, the rift with this branch of the family had acquired a more serious foundation. It dated from the year 1905, when Grand Duke Cyril, the eldest son of Marie Pavlovna and Grand Duke Vladimir, had married abroad without obtaining that legal pre-requisite, the Tsar's consent. What made his offence even more grievous was the fact that his wife, the Grand Duchess Victoria Melita of Saxe–Coburg–Gotha ('Ducky'), was in the first place his cousin (and Russian law prohibited marriages between cousins) and, secondly, the former wife of Alexandra's brother, the Grand Duke of Hesse–Darmstadt, whom she had divorced specifically for this purpose. Nicholas took a very hard line on this occasion, banishing Cyril from the country. Uncle Vladimir was furious and never forgave his nephew – even after Cyril and his wife were allowed to return in 1910. A similar break occurred with another of the Tsar's uncles, the Grand Duke Paul, who contracted a morganatic marriage abroad in 1902 with Madame von Pistohlkors, the divorced wife of one of Grand Duke Vladimir's *aides-de-camp*. In this case, the Tsar imposed the maximum punishment: exile for life. Although this couple too were later permitted to return and the title of Princess Paley was bestowed upon the lady, the bitterness and enmity never disap-peared, and the Princess found the Court of Marie Pavlovna more welcoming and more congenial than that of the Tsarina.

Only Anna Vrubova, as Princess R—— so rightly says, was intimate with Alexandra – but this intimacy was very great and, in the eyes of some onlookers, undesirable. Anna, a daughter of the noble Taniev family, first met the Tsarina when Alexandra visited her when she had typhoid in 1901, at the age of seventeen. Two years later she received from the Empress the diamond-studded *chiffre* of a maid-of-honour and in 1905 was appointed a *Fräulein* in the Tsarina's personal suite. In 1907, after Anna's disastrous marriage had broken up, the final stage in the friend-ship between the two women was reached. Anna was settled in a small, uncomfortable house at Tsarskoe Selo. It did not have stone foundations but rested directly on the frozen earth. It was therefore frequently so cold in winter that when Anna enter-tained Nicholas and Alexandra to 'tea' (to which the Empress contributed the fruit and her husband his favourite drink, cherry brandy), they all had to sit curled up with their feet on the sofa for warmth. Nicholas would plunge into a hot bath to restore his circulation immediately he got back home, so intense was the cold. The austerity of the house was relieved by various gifts from Alexandra – charming pictures and six exquisitely embroidered antique chairs – and when the silver-laden tea-table was brought in, Anna felt that it looked quite cosy.

She became an almost daily visitor at the nearby Alexander Palace, spending afternoons singing duets with Alexandra, her soprano voice mingling with the Empress's contralto; evenings listening to Nicholas reading aloud from Tolstoy, Turgenev or his favourite Gogol; sticking photographs into the green-bound albums with the whole family. So enthusiastic were they about photography that an expert photographer was permanently employed by the household, solely to print and develop their work. Anna even joined them on their yachting trips and holidays. Most of all, she was an active and enthusiastic participant in their experiments in mysticism.

Neither Anna's intellectual prowess nor her physical appearance gave any clue as to why she alone could penetrate the closed world of the imperial family. Monsieur Paléologue observed: 'her thick, gleaming hair, narrow skull, fat, red neck, clammy back, huge thighs – a mound of warm and ample flesh', and was horrified to think that anyone 'so thoroughly mediocre, so lacking in principle and mental refinement, can have any influence in times like these on the destinies of Russia'. Prince Felix Youssoupov recalls her as a young girl whom he used to meet at the regular, very colourful dances held on Saturday evenings at her parents' home. She was tall and stout even then, 'with a puffy, shiny face and no charm whatever. Although she was not at all intelligent, she was extremely crafty and rather shy. It was quite a problem to find partners for her. . . .'

It was typical of the seclusion which Nicholas and Alexandra yearned for that, when in Tsarskoe Selo, it was in the smaller Alexander Palace, hidden by trees amid a park studded with artificial lakes, that they chose to live, and not the Great Palace at the top of the hill, filled with the glamorous ghosts of Catherine II and her entourage. In an open space before the park stood the Feodorovsky Sobor, a little medieval-style church with a charming cupola, one of Alexandra's favourite places.

In the Alexander Palace the Tsar and his wife occupied the ground floor of one wing, and their children the floor above. It would not have lacked charm, Prince Felix comments, 'had it

not been for the young Tsarina's unfortunate improvements'. Apparently, she replaced most of the paintings, stucco ornaments and *bas reliefs* by mahogany woodwork and 'cosy corners'. New furniture by Maples was sent out from England. Alexandra however, thought it delightful and was particularly fond of her opal-hued boudoir. Here, amid hangings of mauve silk, surrounded by vases of fresh roses and lilac, she lay on lace-covered cushions on a low couch, a lace cover lined with mauve silk over her knees, beneath her favourite picture: a large painting of the Holy Virgin asleep, surrounded by angels. Within easy reach stood a small table stacked with books, photos, letters, telegrams and papers in delicious disorder. Nicholas, too, liked this room and spent most of his leisure there, though he did have his own very fine suite consisting of study, sitting- and billiard-rooms and a dressing-room with a swimming bath.

Life followed a very unsophisticated pattern. Ministers and senior officials arrived with reports, and ambassadors were received in audience and invited to lunch, but otherwise the imperial family entertained hardly at all. In keeping with Russian tradition, the Palace had no dining-room, and the table was laid for meals in whichever room was most convenient – sometimes even the library. For the children, existence was almost austere. They slept in large, airy nurseries on hard camp

An informal picture of the imperial family taking tea at Tsarskoe Selo, a few days before the outbreak of war. Anna Vrubova is in the foreground.

The Tsarina's room in the Alexander Palace at Tsarskoe Selo.

beds with no pillows and a minimal ration of blankets. They were subjected to cold baths every morning and allowed hot ones only in the evening before they went to bed. They began lessons with their tutors at nine o'clock in the morning, only taking a break between eleven and twelve for a short drive in a carriage, sledge or car. Then work was resumed until their father, his *aide-de-camp* and an occasional guest joined them for lunch at one. Two hours in the afternoon were spent walking in the open air, when the Tsar, if he were free, would join the young party. He would take part in their games, building ice-hills by the artificial lakes, sliding down them, laboriously climbing up again, and playing with the children's animals, such as Vanka, his son's donkey, or Joy, the silky pet spaniel. Tea marked a high-point in the children's day. The girls were dressed in fresh white frocks and coloured sashes and joined their parents round the little white-draped table gleaming with the silver service and the tea-glasses in silver holders. The routine never varied. Even the food was the same from day to day: hot bread and butter and a few English biscuits. The only alteration was made during Lent when bowls of nuts replaced the other delicacies.

In the late afternoon, lessons were resumed; often the Tsarina would come in and listen while her children were being taught. Although dinner in the evenings was never a ceremonial meal, and if there were any guests at all, they were relatives or family friends, Alexandra always changed into a formal and elaborate gown and wore her jewels. At 9 p.m. without fail, she tiptoed upstairs to tuck her son up for the night.

After dinner, the Tsar would work in his study, a small room with only one window. It was plainly but comfortably furnished with leather chairs, a sofa covered with a Persian rug, a bureau and shelves arranged with meticulous care, a table spread with maps, and a low bookcase with photographs, busts and family souvenirs on the top shelf. It would be far into the night before he would tiptoe along the small passage that separated his study from their bedroom. Unlike many couples in exalted positions at the time, not only did Nicholas and Alexandra share a bedroom, but they also slept in the same bed.

It had been a love match from the start. The young Grand Duke Nicholas had been desperate to marry the beautiful German Princess Alix of Hesse–Darmstadt and had spent many hours of anguish until she had accepted him. Their love had grown and blossomed as the years advanced – even after many years, a blush would spread over her face when she heard the whistle like a bird-call by which her husband summoned her, and she would hasten to join him. Yet ill-fortune seemed to dog their union. It had begun inauspiciously. Alexandra had come in haste to Russia to attend the funeral of her fiancé's father, Alexander III. Their wedding took place within the period of Court mourning because the youthful Tsar could not bear to assume the responsibility of his new rôle alone. Their coronation in May 1895, too, was the occasion of a disaster. A celebration arranged for the common people in a field in Hodynka near Moscow resulted in hundreds of deaths as thousands of men, women and children broke down barriers, and the police were helpless in the face of a general stampede. 'She has come to us behind a coffin', the people muttered. 'She brings misfortune with her.'

Misfortune certainly seemed inseparable from poor Alexandra, although for the next few years it was not immediately apparent. Following her marriage, she gave birth to four daughters: Olga, Tatiana, Marie and Anastasia. It was not until 12 August 1904 that an heir to the throne appeared. He was a

In her youth, the
Tsarina Alexandra had
been a beautiful woman.

very beautiful baby, chubby, with rosy cheeks and golden curls.
The proud parents held him up for all to see. General Mossolov,
head of the Court Chancellery, was allowed to pick him up after
his bath. It was only later that it was discovered that he was
suffering from that dread disease so prevalent among Queen
Victoria's male descendants: haemophilia.

From that moment on, Alexandra never had a moment's peace
of mind. Every time the little Tsarevich Alexis bumped himself,
fell over, or grazed his knee, there was a possibility that internal
bleeding would occur and serious illness ensue. On several
occasions, what would have been a normal and insignificant

178

mishap in an ordinary child brought Alexis to the brink of death. Little wonder that this desperate anxiety reduced his mother, never in any case a particularly robust woman, to a state of high nervous tension if not of actual illness (she was, it was said, suffering from heart trouble) and made her view the frivolities and superficial satisfactions of social life with distaste – quite apart from the fact that she was by nature shy and retiring, and, as a foreigner, had never been fully accepted by Russian Court circles. When she had first arrived in the country, she had been amazed by the idleness of the Russian Court and had formed a society from among its female members who were dedicated to sewing garments for the poor. The society had failed, and Alexandra, older now, sadder and wiser, had ceased her attempts at reform and was content to reject.

The young Alexis had painfully reached the age of ten that winter of 1913–14 when, following the tercentenary celebrations, the whole family retired to the estate at Livadia in the Crimea. It occupied nearly half the peninsula and had, as far as possible, been left in an almost natural condition of vast unbroken forests, wild mountains and valleys. So anxious was the Tsar to keep it this way that for many years he refused to allow that new invention, the motor-car, anywhere in the Crimea. Only much later did he instruct Prince Vladimir Orlov to purchase two or three cars for the imperial garage.

This estate was one of Alexandra's favourite places. The old palace there had been pulled down and a new one built in Italian style amid beautiful gardens and surrounded by superb scenery. Every window in this new palace framed a panorama of the Black Sea. Here, the Tsarina could really rest, lying for hours on her balcony and joining the rest of the family only after luncheon in the central courtyard built after the design of the cloisters of San Marco in Florence. Here, the rest of the family could lead a simple and informal life. They walked and rode and bathed in the sea. They roamed the woods, gathering wild berries and mushrooms which they cooked over open fires for tea. The Tsar and his suite hunted a little, rode a great deal and played tennis of a professional standard. Every Saturday evening there were cinema shows in the covered riding-school. Madame Narishkin, Mistress of the Robes, acted as censor to ensure that the programme was suitable; it usually consisted of a news film of the week's events, taken by the Court photographer, an educational film or a series of attractive views, and then something

A photograph taken by the Tsarina of the new Italianate palace at Livadia in the Crimea. Here, the imperial family could relax and ride, swim and hunt amidst breathtakingly beautiful scenery.

amusing to entertain the children. There was also quite an active social life in the neighbourhood as nearly all the other members of the imperial family as well as many of the aristocracy had villas along the coast. Alexandra busied herself with local good works. She re-equipped TB sanatoria, using money from her own private purse, and organized large bazaars to raise funds to help needy patients. The Tsarina and her ladies worked very hard for these bazaars, and she herself always presided over her own table, selling needlework, embroidery and *objets d'art*, to the delight of Crimean society. One day every summer, designated 'White Flower Day', the imperial ladies actually went out into the streets to sell flowers for charity and for these hospitals.

They stayed for only a short while in Livadia in the winter of 1913–14 and were back in Tsarskoe Selo on 3 January 1914. They returned to Livadia on 5 April, for another period of respite before taking off again, this time to Constanza in Romania

on a one-day State Visit. They sailed on the royal yacht *Standart*, the setting of many of their summer pleasure-trips. Built in Denmark and considered the most perfect boat of its time in the world, the yacht was fitted with every comfort and luxury known to modern science. It was painted black, with a gilded bowsprit and stern. The imperial family's rooms on board were nearly as large as their apartments in their summer villa at Peterhof and were upholstered in pretty light-coloured chintzes. The Tsarina could rest on a couch on deck, while, on normal expeditions, the Tsar could go ashore for a walk or a game of tennis. Their son was cared for by a big, good-natured sailor, Derevanko, who had taught him to walk when he was small and who carried him about when he was ill. Happy evenings were spent by Nicholas and a friend (sometimes General Alexander Orlov) playing billiards, while Alexandra and Anna Vrubova read or sewed.

On this occasion in the summer of 1914, however, there was

The Tsar and his children seem to be enjoying life aboard the imperial yacht *Standart*.

a serious purpose to the trip. It was hoped that a marriage could
be arranged between the Grand Duchess Olga and Prince Carol
of Romania. In the event, Olga did not agree to the proposed
match, but the day spent in Constanza was filled with pomp and
ceremony and left Alexandra completely exhausted. It began as
the *Standart* docked, and the whole Romanian royal family were
on the landing-stage at Constanza to meet them. There followed
a State drive through the town, a service at the Cathedral and a
family luncheon party. In the afternoon, the Tsarina gave a tea
party on the *Standart* for Romanian royalty and officials, and in
the evening there was a State dinner at the palace. After a fire-

The Tsar and Tsarevich
inspect the crew of
the streamlined,
ultra-modern *Standart*.

works display and a torchlight procession, the imperial family finally returned to the *Standart* at about midnight.

Such visits played a large part in the lives of Nicholas and Alexandra. Many of them, however, could be regarded not as State occasions but as family reunions. Between them, they were related to a large number of the crowned heads of Europe. Alexandra was a grand-daughter of Queen Victoria: Nicholas's mother was the sister of Queen Alexandra of England; both, then, were cousins of George V of England (whom they liked) and Kaiser Wilhelm of Germany (who was by no means regarded with affection).

The family spent most of the summer of 1914 at Peterhof, where they inhabited a small, unpretentious villa, the Alexandra Cottage, at the seaside. It stood in the centre of a wooded park away from the complex of palatial residences which Peter the Great had constructed. Ignoring the Great Palace as well as Marly and Mon Plaisir, Peter's villa on the very edge of the sea, Nicholas and Alexandra lived in two small brick buildings connected by a covered bridge. The rooms were simply furnished, some of them in the English style. The Tsar's study on the first floor, with windows overlooking the Gulf of Finland, was furnished solely with a couple of tables, a settee, six leather chairs and a few engravings of military subjects.

The sun shone brightly in those delightful spring days and a holiday spirit pervaded the whole party. On 8 May, for example, the Tsar decided to take his son out for the day. They drove in a car through the beautiful pine forests on the slopes of the Jaila mountains till they reached 'Red Rock'. At one point they stopped the car, and Alexis had tremendous fun frolicking in the snow, while his father beamed benignly.

What greater contrast could there have been to the scene in St Petersburg on 2 August. The crowds in the city streets were unbelievable as the Tsar and his family drove to the Winter Palace. They were packed so tightly that it seemed that anyone in the city who had legs able to support him had staggered forth to be with his sovereign on that day. The imperial motor-cars could barely move through the dense mass of people. At a snail's pace they managed to progress from the quay to the palace while the onlookers cheered themselves hoarse, sang the national anthem and called down the blessing of God on their sovereign. The imperial cortege was able, with the assistance of the police, to reach the Winter Palace, but many of the Tsar's suite were

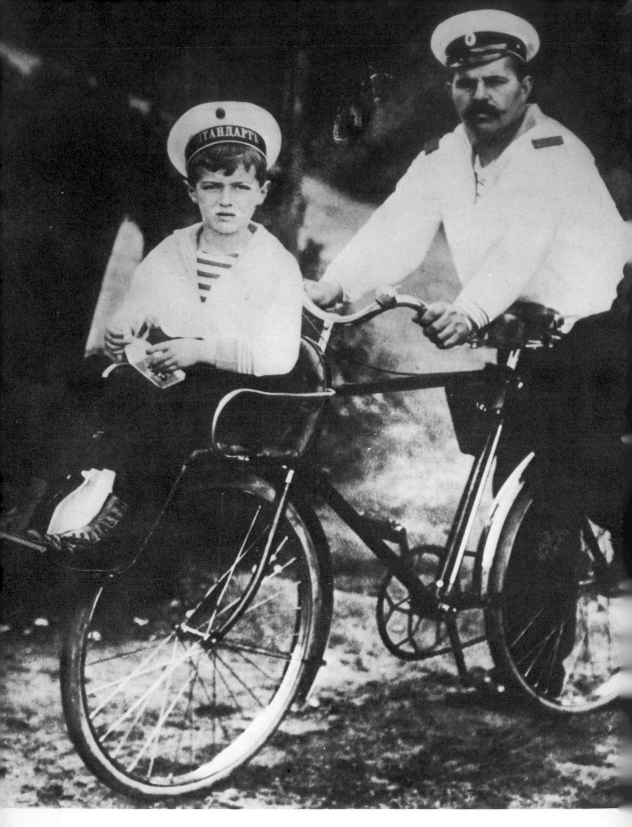

184

prevented by the crowds from entering the great square in front
of the palace and had to be escorted through a side door opening
from the small garden to the west.

Within, five or six thousand people were assembled in the
vast Salle de Nicholas, 200 feet long by 61 feet broad, with
sixteen windows running along the Neva quay, to hear a solemn
Te Deum Mass. The whole Court was in full dress, and all the
officers of the garrison were in field dress. Standing before a
table bearing the miraculous ikon of the Virgin of Kazan,
Nicholas took the traditional oath, 'I solemnly swear that I will
never make peace so long as one of the enemy is on the soil of the
fatherland.' A violent outburst of cheering lasting for almost ten

minutes greeted this announcement. For several hours, Tsar and Tsarina stood and received tokens of homage from thousands of officials, ministers and members of the nobility. As they moved slowly through the crowds, men and women threw themselves on their knees, kissing their hands with tears in their eyes. Vast crowds were gathered in the Winter Palace square carrying flags and ikons and portraits of the Tsar. As Nicholas appeared on the balcony with Alexandra and little Alexis at his side, the entire crowd sank to their knees in one spontaneous movement and sang the Russian national anthem, 'God Save the Tsar'. To them, in the words of Paléologue, 'the Tsar was really the autocrat appointed of God, the military, political and religious leader of his people, the absolute master of their bodies and souls'.

On 18 August the scene was repeated in the St George's Hall of the Kremlin Palace in Moscow. The high dignitaries of the empire, the ministers and delegates of the nobility, the middle classes and the merchant community, rose to silent attention as, promptly on the stroke of eleven, the Tsar, the Tsarina and the imperial family made a ceremonial entry. The inevitable Cossack carried the Tsarevich, who had hurt his leg the previous day. Then the Tsar, in a full, firm voice, addressed the people of Moscow. He had come, he said, as the traditions of his ancestors decreed, to seek the moral support he needed in prayer at the relics in the Kremlin. He declared that a heroic national impulse was sweeping over all Russia, without distinction of race or nationality. Prolonged cheering greeted his final statement: 'From this place, the very heart of Russia, I send my soul's greetings to my valiant troops and my noble allies. God is with us!'

The party then passed through the St Vladimir Room and the Sacred Gallery, descended the Red Staircase and crossed a bridge with a purple awning to reach the Ouspensky Sobor. Paléologue describes the scene:

This edifice is square, surmounted by a gigantic dome supported by four massive pillars, and all its walls are covered with frescoes in a gilded background. The ikonostasis, a lofty screen, is one mass of precious stones. The dim light falling from the cupola and the flickering glow of the candles kept the nave in a ruddy semi-darkness.

The Tsar and Tsarina stood in front of the right ambo [pulpit] at the foot of the column against which the throne of the Patriarchs is set.

186

In the left ambo the Court choir, in sixteenth-century silver and light blue costume, chanted the beautiful anthems of the Orthodox rite, perhaps the finest anthems in sacred music.

At the end of the nave, opposite the ikonostasis, the three Metropolitans of Russia and twelve archbishops stood in line. In the aisles on the left was a group of one hundred and ten bishops, archimandrites and abbots. A fabulous, indescribable wealth of diamonds, sapphires, rubies and amethysts sparkled on the brocade of their mitres and chasubles. At the time the church glowed with a supernatural light.

Tsar and Tsarina reverently kissed a crucifix said to contain a portion of the true cross and then walked round the cathedral to kneel at the relics and tombs of the patriarchs. The ceremony was over. Out in the open, a great cheer burst forth from the bare-headed crowd, and every bell in Moscow broke into song.

'This is a sublime moment to have lived to see!' the British Ambassador whispered to his French counterpart. 'Think of all the historic future being made here and now.'

8 The Numbered Days

Russia on the morrow of the declaration of war was a solemn, sober country, inspired by a spirit of intense patriotism. Society ladies hastened to enlist as nurses in the hospitals set up for the troops, and the wives of rich merchants vied with each other in giving money to endow these hospitals. Gala performances were held in state theatres to raise funds for the Red Cross, and audiences at places of entertainment stood tensely to attention as the orchestra played the national anthems of the allied nations, France, Britain and Russia, at the end of performances. All differences were forgotten. All opposing factions were united in a common cause. The Duma held a short one-day session on 26 July 1914 and promised the government unconditional support. The Zemstvo assembly in Moscow declared: 'Gone now are the barriers which have divided our citizens; all are joined in one common effort.'

The wave of patriotism continued unabated during the first months of the war, encouraged by Russian victories which followed one after another and undiminished by the news of French defeats on the Western Front. Bruce-Lockhart recalls a gala performance in Moscow on 10 September 1914, in honour of the capture of Lemberg, when unexpectedly there was also a French victory to celebrate. The play was an adaptation of Rostand's *L'Aiglon*. The theatre was a blaze of colour, with the uniforms of the officers forming a brilliant setting for the jewels and fine dresses of the ladies. When the curtain had fallen at the end of the first act, the footlights went up, the orchestra filed in,

. . . and a young girl of eighteen, the daughter of the President of the French Chamber of Commerce, came on to the stage. With her white dress, her face free of all make-up, and her glorious golden hair, she looked like the Angel Gabriel. In her trembling hands she held a slip of paper.

The audience hushed itself in an expectant silence. Then, quivering with emotion and nervousness, the girl began to read: 'The following official telegram has just been received from French headquarters.' She stopped as if her tongue were chained. The tears streamed down her face.

Then in a shrill crescendo, she read the message: '*Je suis heureux de vous annoncer victoire sur tout le front – Joffre.*'

The lights blazed up. The girl ran wildly off the stage, and in a storm of cheering the orchestra struck up the 'Marseillaise'. Bearded men kissed each other. Women smiled and wept at the same time. Then, as the orchestra broke into the chorus, a miracle happened.

PREVIOUS PAGES
Russian soldiers demonstrate against the continuance of the war, 1917.

ЦАРСТВУЙ НА СТРАХЪ ВРАГАМЪ

ФОТО В-БОНИЦЪ-РИГА-1914.г.   ·ПЕРЕПЕЧАТКА ВОСПРЕЩАЕТСЯ (ЗАКОНЪ ОТЪ 20 МАРТА 1911 г. СТ.59.П.1.) ДОЗВ.ПРИДВ.ЦЕНЗ

From the gallery above came the tramp of marching feet, and four hundred French reservists, singing in a glorious unison, took up the refrain. . . . It was the last occasion on which Russia was to feel supremely confident about the outcome of the war.

A patriotic postcard of the Tsar, printed and sent before massive defeats and food and munitions shortages had dampened Russian enthusiasm.

Bruce-Lockhart was right. Russia had already suffered one major defeat at Tannenberg in August 1914, when she had prematurely launched an offensive to divert German troops from the French front. She had lost the cream of her fighting force on this occasion. During the ensuing months and years, defeat followed hard on defeat, interspersed by only the occasional victory. The number of Russian war dead exceeded the wildest imagination. The Russian army was the victim of every variety of bungling and maladministration. Worst of all, it was rendered almost completely ineffectual by a desperate shortage of ammunition. Industrial production had increased greatly in the first decades of the twentieth century, but it had not increased enough, and the conscription of factory workers had put an additional strain on it. Similarly, although Russia had made a tremendous effort to catch up with the West in railway building after a delayed start, her railway system was grossly inadequate

Scenes of rejoicing in the Nevsky Prospect in St Petersburg after the news of Russian victory at Przemysl.

for the movement of troops and of food supplies over her vast expanses.

At home, shortages of food supplies were also apparent – caused not only by the deficiencies in the transport system but also by the decrease in production, as millions of peasants were removed from the land and pressed into the army; by the virtual absence of many imported items from the market; and by the corruption and ineptitude of some minor officials concerned in distribution. Moreover demand had increased, as the army fed its peasant soldiers at a higher level than they had previously fed themselves. In St Petersburg (renamed Petrograd on 1 September 1914) and Moscow, queues formed outside food shops to buy the bare necessities at prices few could afford.

Rumours flew through the cities, and anti-German feeling ran high. In June 1915 serious riots broke out in Moscow. Any shop or factory or even private house belonging to anyone with a German-sounding name was attacked by the mob, looted, sometimes burned to the ground. Piano shops were particularly vulnerable, and bonfires were made of many a worthy Bechstein and Blüthner. The country house of Knop, the great Russo–German cotton millionaire, was razed to the ground. It took the police three days and many bullets to restore order. What is more, gossip seized on the German origins of the Tsarina Alexandra to associate her with the outburst of popular emotion. At best, she was attributed with pro-German sympathies. At worst, it was suggested that she was working hand-in-glove with the German authorities to bring about Russian defeat and a German victory. Various stories circulating at the time pressed home the message. For example, the Tsarevich was said to have been found weeping in a corridor of the Winter Palace. 'What's the matter, sonny?' asked a visiting general. 'Well, you see,' replied the Tsarevich, 'when the Russians are beaten, my father cries. When the Germans lose a battle, my mother cries. When am I to cry?' Anti-German feeling reached its height in January 1916, when the highly unpopular Boris Stürmer, a *protégé* of Rasputin's, replaced the aged Goremykin as Chairman of the Council of Ministers. Bernard Pares quotes an anonymous verse of the time which reflects the state of popular tempers:

> Fresh comes Stürmer from the Palace
> In his diplomatic role.
> *Deutschland, Deutschland über Alles!*
> *Russland, Russland, lebe wohl!*
>
> Friend of Russia's bold freemasons,
> Cursing Petrograd and all,
> See how Lord Sazonov hastens
> To his Finnish waterfall.
>
> 'Stürmer, Stürmer, very shocking!'
> Mutters Grey in far Hyde Park.
> 'He may say he is Nashchokin;
> I suspect he'll be Bismarck.'
>
> 'Not for nought he looks a villain
> Fur as red as fox – the pup!
> And exactly like friend William,
> His moustachios twisted up.'

As he dines with dames of fashions
'Ah, the future's full of fog,'
Ruminates in deep depression
Our poor Monsieur Paléologue.

'Seems as if our work's undone:
New appointments – very strange.'
So Buchanan writes to London
On the ministerial change.

'Shall we run upon the shallows?
Does it sound our friendship's knell?
Deutschland, Deutschland über Alles!
England, England, fare thee well!'

In their graves will shake with malice,
And above the bells will toll:
Deutschland, Deutschland, über Alles!
Russland, Russland, lebe wohl!

Public opinion, never kindly disposed towards Alexandra, was gradually turning to genuine enmity. It was true that the Tsarina had thrown herself heart and soul into nursing the moment war was declared. Together with her two elder daughters, she diligently embarked on the requisite course of practical and theoretical training. All three duly sat and passed their examinations at the end of the course and worked day and night in the wards, taking their fair share of the duties involved in caring for the thousands upon thousands of wounded and dying soldiers brought in an endless stream of ambulances to the cities. She also initiated several *sklads*, workshops to prepare linen and bandages for the hospitals. She organized 'bath trains' to be sent to remote areas of the front line. She was tireless in visiting hospitals and nursing centres in her hours off duty. . . .

But, as she once said herself, nothing she ever did was right in Russian eyes. There were even complaints when she appeared in public in nurse's uniform. It was not fitting for an empress so to dress, it was said. Greatest protests, however, were aroused by the increasing ascendancy that Rasputin was obtaining, or was said to be obtaining, over the imperial couple. This was particularly the case as Rasputin, even before the commencement of hostilities, had pronounced his opposition to the war. 'Fear, fear War', he was quoted as saying. 'The Balkans are not worth fighting about.' While he was still recovering from his stab wounds, he sent a telegram to Anna Vrubova: 'Let Papa not plan

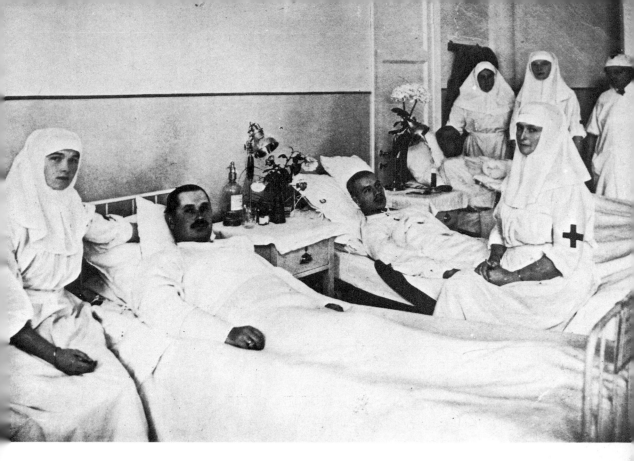

war, for with war will come the end of Russia and yourselves, and you will lose to the last man.' Even in 1915 he was quoted as saying:

Russia entered this war against the will of God. Evil be to those who still refuse to believe it! To hear the voice of God, all that is necessary is to listen humbly. But when men are strong, they are puffed up with pride: they think themselves clever and despise the simple until one day the judgment of God falls upon them like a thunderclap. Christ is angry at all the groans that mount to him from the soil of Russia. But what do *they* care, the generals, about having *moujiks* killed; it doesn't prevent them eating or drinking or getting rich. . . . Alas! the blood of the victims will not bespatter them alone: it will bespatter the Tsar himself for he is the father of the *moujiks*. . . . I tell you, the vengeance of God will be terrible!

The people, already criticizing Alexandra for lack of enthusiasm in the fight against Germany, saw Rasputin's pacifist approach as a highly dangerous influence.

Nor did Rasputin's general conduct improve his image. He brought off wonderful triumphs of mystical achievement – and

The Tsarina and her two eldest daughters Olga and Tatiana nursing wounded soldiers in the Imperial Hospital at Tsarskoe Selo. In spite of her efforts to support the Russian cause, public opinion remained firmly against the German-born Tsarina and was convinced that she was avidly pro-German.

almost simultaneously, he would commit debaucheries of undisguised squalor. On 15 January 1915, for example, Anna Vrubova was involved in a serious train disaster outside Tsarskoe Selo. A heavy iron girder fell on her head and pinned her down, so that she was rescued only with difficulty. On the Tsarina's orders, she was carried on a stretcher improvised from a compartment door to the hospital of Princess Gedroitz near by. Anna had sustained grievous injuries. Her skull and spine had been damaged, her right leg crushed and her left broken in two places. She was given up for dead. In her delirium, she cried continuously, 'Father Gregory, pray for me!' Holy Communion was delivered and the imperial couple were standing by her bed, when Rasputin himself, summoned post-haste from Petrograd, entered the room. He fixed the suffering patient with his calm, pale blue eyes. 'Annushka, wake up! Look at me!' he commanded. Miraculously, Anna's eyes opened slowly: 'Gregory! That's you! Thank God.' 'She will recover,' Rasputin pronounced, 'but she will remain a cripple.' Then he staggered from the room as if exhausted from the spiritual strength he had expended, and collapsed in a dead faint.

Rasputin's prophecies in this instance were correct. Anna recovered. She remained a cripple. His prestige was considerably enhanced by this incident. It was unfortunate that, only four months later, he was involved in a major scandal. Bruce-Lockhart was present in the Yar restaurant in Petrovsky Park, one of the most luxurious night haunts of Moscow, on 8 April 1915. He was watching a cabaret performance in the main room when suddenly a violent disturbance broke out in one of the private rooms.

Wild shrieks of women, a man's curses, broken glass and the banging of doors raised a discordant pandemonium. Head waiters rushed upstairs. The manager sent for the policeman who was always on duty at such establishments. But the row and the roaring continued. There was more coming and going of waiters and policemen, and scratching of heads and holding of councils. The cause of the disturbance was Rasputin – drunk and lecherous.

He was finally removed snarling and vowing vengeance and with his clothes in a disarray that contemporary observers could only describe as grossly indecent.

A year later Rasputin had another triumph. In December 1915 the Tsar was leaving with his son for a trip to inspect the southern front, when Alexis's nose began to bleed. The mild bleeding developed into a haemorrhage. The Tsarevich repeatedly lost consciousness, and his life was twice despaired of. The Tsar, in desperation, ordered that the imperial train return to Tsarskoe Selo. The Tsarina was warned and immediately rushed to Rasputin for help. He bowed his head in solemn prayer. 'Thanks be to God! He has given me your son's life once more', he reported. The next day, 18 December, when the train bearing the invalid reached Tsarskoe, his condition showed a startling improvement. But the following month Rasputin was involved in another unsavoury incident in a notorious Petrograd gipsy dive, the Villa Rode.

Rasputin's deeds and misdeeds would have had little practical impact if rumour had not connected him so closely with Alexandra, and if the Tsarina herself had not wielded so great a political influence. But Alexandra's devotion to and faith in Rasputin were undoubtedly growing under the impact of his 'miracles', and her husband's prolonged absences at the front gave her great opportunities to influence the Tsar's decisions.

Nicholas, with the old concept of the sovereign as leader of his armies deep in his blood, was with difficulty dissuaded from leading his troops into battle at the start of the war. He finally agreed to compromise by appointing his cousin the Grand Duke Nicholas as Commander-in-Chief and himself establishing a mobile headquarters as near to the front as was compatible with safety. He spent as much time as possible at this *stavka*, taking Alexis with him on several occasions. Paléologue visited him there in March 1915, when it was stationed at Baronovici, a small country town outside Vilna. Here he found a dozen trains arranged in a fan formation in the clearing of a forest. He was received by the Tsar in the drawing-room car of the imperial train, then moved into the dining-room where a table was laid for twenty. Finally, he had a lengthy discussion with the Tsar in the imperial study, a rectangular compartment filled with plain furniture and large leather chairs. On the same visit Paléologue also had talks with the Grand Duke Nicholas, whose train was parked near by. He was taken into a roomy, comfortable apartment spread with bearskins and eastern rugs. He also saw the Commander-in-Chief's luxurious saloon and his light, bright bedroom, with one wall covered completely in ikons.

By August 1915, desolated by the defeats his army was sustaining, Nicholas could stand inactivity no longer. He decided,

The Tsar and
Tsarevich reviewing
the navy in 1916.

against a great deal of advice, to dismiss the Grand Duke and
assume complete control of his armies himself. In vain did members of the imperial family and the foreign diplomatic corps
attempt to dissuade him. Even his own ministers were incensed
– apart from anything else, the decision had been taken without
reference to or consultation with them. It amounted, they felt, to
a vote of no confidence. The majority of them signed a letter to
the Tsar protesting against his projected move. Among other
things, they argued that he, the Tsar, would now be responsible
for any military defeat. Thereafter, anything at all that went
wrong in Russia would be the Tsar's fault. 'The Ministers are
rotten . . . I am more than disgusted with those cowards',
Alexandra wrote to her husband. Nicholas, fully aware of the

implications, had made up his mind: 'Perhaps a scapegoat is needed to save Russia', he is quoted as saying. 'I mean to be the victim. May the will of God be done.' On 3 September Tsar and Tsarina were in Petrograd making their devotions at the Cathedral of the Fortress and at Our Lady of Kazan before he embarked on the momentous step. Few of the ministers who had signed the letter remained in office for long after its receipt.

It was generally assumed that Alexandra and Rasputin had influenced the Tsar's decision. They had, it was said, convinced him that 'when the throne and country are in peril, the post of a Tsar–autocrat is at the head of his armies. To yield that post to another is to disobey the will of God.' Alexandra was also worried about the growing popularity of the Grand Duke

The Tsar–autocrat was convinced that he should personally conduct the war and lead his armies in the field, and was dissuaded from doing so with the utmost difficulty. He is seen here with his retinue in his headquarters at Mogilev.

Nicholas with the armies. In April 1915 she wrote to her husband:

Forgive me . . . but you know you are too kind and gentle . . . be more decided and sure of yourself – you know perfectly well what is right, and when you do not agree and are right, bring your opinion to the front and let it weigh against the rest. They must remember more who you are and that first they must turn to you. Your being charms every single one, but I want you to hold them by your brain and experience. Though Nikolasha is highly placed, you are above him. The same thing shocked our Friend, as me too, that Nikolasha words his telegrams, answers to governors, etc., in your style – his ought to be more simple and humble and other things.

On 15 June she went even further: 'I have absolutely no faith in N. I know him to be far from clever, and having gone against a man of God; his work cannot be blessed, nor his advice be good.' On the other hand, these injunctions may only have been repeating what Nicholas himself wished to hear. He once said, '. . . when I'm worried or doubtful, or vexed, I have only to talk to Gregory for five minutes to feel myself immediately soothed and strengthened. He always manages to say what I need to hear, and the effect of his wise words lasts several weeks.'

Be that as it may, with Nicholas away for increasingly lengthy periods, Alexandra's opportunities to wield the reins of power grew daily. 'Lovey, I am here', she wrote in one of her innumerable letters to her husband at the front. 'Don't laugh at silly old wifey, but she has trousers on unseen. . . .'

Alexandra was truly wearing the trousers, passing on to the Tsar advice and suggestions couched in loving but no less firm terms – and behind her recommendations lay the whispered word of Rasputin. Under their joint guidance, minister succeeded minister in quick succession. Regardless of Russia's desperate situation, of the defeats in battle and of the unrest on the home front, regardless of their efficiency or popularity, those unfavourably disposed to Rasputin were dismissed, to be replaced by men whose support he could depend on. It culminated in October 1916 with the appointment of the reactionary psychopath Protopopov as Minister of the Interior.

With the dismissal of one popular minister after another, taken in conjunction with the disastrous war news and the astronomical figures of Russian dead, dissatisfaction within the country grew daily. It blazed into anger when, on 15 September 1915, the Tsar signed a *ukase* proroguing the Duma, the popular assembly, the only weapon the Russian nation had against the senseless, destructive rule of one man. The possibility of co-operation between government and Duma was now out of the question. Thereafter it was open struggle.

Nonetheless, the Tsar made one last attempt. On 9 February 1916, when the Duma was once more convoked, Nicholas for the first time (and the last) visited it in its chamber at the Tauride Palace. It was a momentous occasion, beginning with a religious service and concluding with set speeches from the Tsar himself, and from Rodzianko. Nicholas, however, was anything but comfortable.

He was very pale, almost livid [Paléologue writes]. His mouth continually tightened, as if he were trying to swallow something. More than ten times he indulged in the family trick and tugged at his collar with his right hand; his left hand, in which he held his gloves and cap, was perpetually opening and closing; his discomfort was obvious enough. . . . [During his speech, he was] quite painful to watch. His voice could hardly struggle through his throat. He stopped or stumbled over every word. His left hand shook violently; his right nervously clutched his belt. The unhappy man was quite out of breath when he reached the conclusion of what he had to say.

Hatred and distrust of the regime continued unabated. It took various forms. With the revolutionary intelligentsia, it was a tool to bring about the eventual overthrow of the autocracy. In exile in Siberia, Switzerland or the United States, the leaders watched closely over the symptoms of impending doom. With many, it was concentrated into an intense hatred of Rasputin, who was seen as the force of every evil besetting Russia. Plots and attempts on his life multiplied.

Haute société did its best to close its eyes to the gravity of the situation. Theatres, ballets and operas continued undeterred. Chaliapin was singing *Don Quixote* at the Narodny Dom. Kschessinska danced *Giselle* at the Maryinsky. Karsavina took the lead in both *Sylvia* and *The Water Lily* at the same theatre.

The sumptuous hall, with its blue and gold hangings, was quite full; the evening marked the opening of the winter season and the resumption of those ballets in which the Russian imagination loves to follow the interplay of flying forms and rhythmic movements through the music. From the stalls to the back row of the highest circle, I could see nothing but a sea of cheery, smiling faces. In the intervals, the boxes came to life with the irresponsible chatter which made the bright eyes of the women sparkle with merriment. Irksome thoughts of the present, sinister visions of war and the melancholy prospects of the future vanished as if by magic the moment the orchestra struck up. An air of pleasant unreality was in every face [wrote Maurice Paléologue].

An anonymous verse dating from the early days of 1916 (again quoted by Pares) depicted the situation:

Our Moods

We do not take defeat amiss,
And victory gives us no delight;
The source of all our cares is this
Can we get vodka for tonight.

The victories we can do without.
No! Peace and quiet is our line,
Intrigues and scandal, evenings out
Trimmed up with women and with wine.

We only want to know next day
What ministers will be on view,
Or who takes who to see the play.
Or who at Cuba's sat next who:

Has Vyrbova had to go?
Or can Kuvaka give you joy?
Or how the Germans knead their dough,
Or why on earth there's Shabhovskoy.

And does Rasputin still prevail?
Or do we need another saint?
And is Kshesinskaya quite well?
And how that feast at Shubin's went.

If the Grand Duke took Dina home
What kind of luck MacDiddie's had —
Oh, if a Zeppelin would come
And smash the whole of Petrograd!

Even official dinners continued to sparkle discordantly. A dinner at the Foreign Office, part of a round of entertainment provoked by an official visit by Prince Kanin, cousin of the Mikado of Japan, in September 1916, elicited the following comments from Paléologue: 'Too much glare, silver and plate, food and music; too many flowers and servants! It was all dazzle

A vicious caricature of Rasputin manipulating the Tsar and Tsarina.

Россійскій царствующій домъ...

and noise. . . .' Three days later there was a brilliant reception for the same guest at the Japanese Embassy, while at the end of October a dinner was held in honour of Baron Motono, Japanese Ambassador to Russia, at the Ministry for Foreign Affairs. The scene here was sumptuous. Potted palms were present in such abundance that the company had the impression of entering a jungle.

In the shops, precisely at that time, Paléologue noted that the price of the most basic necessities was three times above its pre-war level. In fact, wood and eggs were four times as expensive, butter and soap five.

Not all the social élite was content to dance its way through the war. The young, wealthy, handsome Prince Felix Youssoupov had listened intently to the debates in the Duma when Rasputin had been castigated as the cause of all Russia's ills. It made a deep impression on him, and he decided that, for the good of his country, Rasputin must go.

He first set about finding accomplices to assist him in the task and succeeded in enlisting the support of the Grand Duke Dimitri, a childhood friend and son of the Grand Duke Paul, a certain Captain Soukhotin, Dr Stanislas Lazovert and a member of the Duma, Vladimir Pourichkevich. His next step was to gain the acquaintance of Rasputin and win his confidence. Complaining of ill health, he easily convinced the holy man of his need for help and underwent several sessions of treatment that verged closely on hypnosis. From there, it was simple to invite Rasputin to his flat in the house on the Moika, theoretically to meet his wife (though, in reality, Princess Irina was away from home on the date fixed).

Hastily, the flat was furnished with rich hangings and costly vases in preparation for the visit. Prince Felix himself went to the cathedral of Our Lady of Kazan to make his devotions and invoke God's blessing on his action. Back at the flat, Dr Lazovert was sprinkling potassium cyanide crystals on to small iced cakes – enough crystals, he said, to kill several men instantly – and into the bottoms of wine glasses. The whole scene was arranged to give the impression that a party had taken place in the basement and that the guests had retired upstairs to smoke and carouse. To enhance the effect, a record of 'Yankee Doodle' was placed on the gramophone.

Only when everything was ready did Prince Felix depart to fetch his illustrious guest in his motor-car. Dressed in a silk

204

blouse embroidered with cornflowers, a thick raspberry-pink cord at his waist, velvet breeches and well-polished boots, Rasputin accompanied the Prince to the car. He exuded a strong smell of cheap soap, Felix noted. His hair was carefully brushed, and his beard combed. He had obviously dressed carefully for the prospect of meeting the very beautiful Princess Irina.

At the flat, Rasputin at first refused the cakes, 'I don't want any. They're too sweet.' But then, as he ate one after another, Prince Felix watched horrified; the poison should have taken effect immediately. Rasputin also drank several glasses of Madeira, well laced with potassium cyanide. Still nothing happened – except that the holy man appeared to sink into a deep depression and asked his host to entertain him by playing his guitar.

At last, the strain became too much for Felix. At 2.30 a.m., he rushed upstairs where the noise his friends were making indicated that they too were growing impatient. 'The poison hasn't acted', he shouted. Taking Dimitri's revolver, he returned to his guest, who was bending down admiring a crystal crucifix. Without more ado, Felix shot him through the heart. Rasputin gave a violent scream and fell down on a bearskin rug. Hearing these sounds, the conspirators came tumbling down the stairs. The doctor pronounced Rasputin dead.

While arrangements were under way for the disposal of the body, Prince Felix, stirred by who knows what strange doubts, went to inspect it. To his utter horror, he saw first one then the other eye slowly open. Then, foaming at the mouth, Rasputin leapt up roaring and threw himself upon the Prince. Pourichkevich appeared at the moment when Rasputin was disappearing through the door. He fired two shots. Rasputin tottered and fell on the snow.

The shots had alerted the police – never long absent anywhere in imperial Russia. Although Prince Felix explained that he and some friends had been indulging in a little gentle horseplay which had resulted in the shooting of a dog, further inquiries were made, during which Pourichkevich proclaimed: '. . . I am Vladimir Mitrophanovich Pourichkevich, member of the Duma. The shots you heard killed Rasputin. If you love your country and your Tsar, you'll keep your mouth shut. . . .' Meanwhile Dimitri, Soukhotin and Dr Lazovert had wrapped the body in a linen shroud and hurled it into the river from the top of the bridge on Petrovski Island.

The Tsarina, pensive and grief-stricken, and clearly wearing mourning, a short time after Rasputin's assassination.

On 30 December 1916, a soldier crossing Petrovski Bridge saw blood on the snow. After a prolonged search, Rasputin's body was discovered beneath the ice. Excitement in Petrograd was intense, and rumours of every sort were in circulation. Dimitri was arrested and sent off to a small village on the Persian frontier. So incensed were the imperial family by the severity of this sentence, so distressed by the general plight of Russia that they sent a combined petition to Nicholas and Alexandra asking for mercy for Dimitri and pointing to the dire peril to which the Tsar's policy at home was exposing the country and the dynasty. But it was to no avail. Their petition was peremptorily refused. Nicholas was a coffin-bearer at Rasputin's simple funeral in the park at Tsarskoe Selo. Alexandra and Alexis followed the bier. Daily, for weeks after the funeral, the Tsarina and Anna Vrubova went quietly to pray at the grave.

Dimitri had killed Rasputin to save Russia. It is an irony of history that his action had the reverse effect. Deprived of their

principal adviser and spiritual guide, Nicholas and Alexandra did not know which way to turn. The Tsar seemed like a lost soul, dazed, a man who had lost his grasp of the situation; when Paléologue went to see him on 7 January 1917. He too seemed to be recalling, as people throughout the country were recalling, a prophecy which Rasputin had made to the imperial couple: 'If I die or you desert me, you will lose your son and your crown within six months.'

Already that January, people were talking about the possibility of an abdication; already there were rumours that some of the guards regiments forming the garrison of Petrograd were wavering in their loyalty to their Tsar and might be prepared to participate in a plot to force him to renounce the throne. While *haute société* in the capital wined and dined, while champagne flowed freely in dining-rooms and clubs, queues formed outside the bakers' shops as the hungry people waited all night for deliveries that never came in the morning. In one of the coldest

Ill-commanded and under-equipped, many Russian troops deserted in 1916–17.

Violence on the
Petrograd streets in
July 1917, when the
Bolsheviks organized
a demonstration
against the provisional
government.

winters ever, fuel was virtually unobtainable, and even the
embassy staff shivered as central heating systems failed.

On 29 January 1917 French, British and Italian delegates to
an allied conference arrived in Petrograd to discuss the course
of the war. They were entertained to a wild round of luncheons,
receptions and dinners at the embassies, the Finance Ministry,
the Franco–Russian Chamber of Commerce, the President of
the Council's residence, the Town Council, the Grand Duchess
Marie Pavlovna's palace, the Yacht Club and so on – starting
with a State Banquet at the Alexander Palace. The menu –
consisting of *Potage crême d'orge; Fruites glâcées de Gatchina;
Longe de veau Marengo; Poulets de grains rôtis; Salade de*

The Tsar depicted wallowing in the blood of the Russian people, surrounded by symbols of death.

concombres; Glâce maniarine – was adapted to the exigencies of wartime. Otherwise, the magnificent plate, the brilliant livery and the whole glittering display of an imperial function were present in full.

The allied missions had impressed on the Tsar the urgent need for Russia to pursue the war with unimpaired if not increased zeal. Nicholas had reiterated his intention so to do. But to the people of Russia the war had become an abomination, an ordeal of mass slaughter, hardship and starvation. On 8 March 1917 processions thronged the streets of Petrograd shouting 'Bread and Peace!' and singing the '*Marseillaise*'. The riots shared equal place in society's conversation with a party which

Soldiers at the Front welcome the news of the Revolution with wild enthusiasm.

Princess Leon Radziwill was scheduled to throw the following Sunday. It promised to be exceptionally brilliant, with music and dancing after supper.

Day after day the demonstrations continued. On 12 March Paléologue looked out of his window and saw a mob approaching the Alexandra Bridge carrying red flags. From the other end, a regiment of guards was advancing. Fascinated, the French Ambassador waited for the inevitable clash. 'On the contrary,' he wrote, 'the two bodies coalesced. The army was fraternizing with revolt.' Shortly afterwards he heard that the Volhynian regiment of the guard had mutinied during the night, killed its officers and was marching through the streets of the city inciting the people to join the revolt.

The revolution had begun. The bodies who jointly assumed power – the Executive Committee of the Duma and the Council of Working Men and Soldier Deputies, the Soviet – were agreed on a decision that the monarchy must be retained but that

Nicholas II, who was responsible for the current disasters, must be sacrificed to the salvation of Russia. The spontaneous renunciation of the throne by Nicholas II is the only means of saving the imperial system and the dynasty of the Romanovs, they declared. It was ultimately resolved that the Tsar must abdicate the throne in favour of the Tsarevich, who would rule with the Grand Duke Michael as regent.

On 14 March 1917 Nicholas was hastening home to Tsarskoe Selo, where the Tsarina was nursing the children through an acute attack of measles. The imperial train was stopped at Pskov, half-way between Petrograd and Dvinsk. Two members of the Duma boarded it. The following day, with dignity and resignation, the Tsar signed a decree of abdication in favour of his brother Michael. He had felt it impossible to part with his son. On 16 March Michael himself abdicated.

The way was open for the fulfilment of another of Rasputin's prophecies: 'I can see heaps, masses of corpses, several Grand Dukes and hundreds of Counts. . . . The Neva will be all red with blood.'

EPILOGUE

On 30 July 1918 the White Army entered the Bolshevik-held industrial town of Ekaterinburg in Siberia. Immediately, a party of officers set off for a house which had once belonged to an engineer called Ipatiev. It was known to have been occupied by 'Citizen Romanov' and his household since April 1918.

They found the Ipatiev house empty when they burst through the high stockade surrounding it. The sole occupant was a wretched spaniel howling with hunger. It bore a striking resemblance to Joy, the Tsarevich's pet. They searched the house from top to bottom and in the basement noted certain ominous details: the floor had recently been thoroughly scoured and the walls were scarred by bullets. Of the imperial family there was no sign.

In January 1919 Nicholas Sokolov was appointed by the White Government in Siberia to investigate their disappearance. With the assistance of the Tsarevich's erstwhile tutors, Pierre Gilliard and Sidney Gibbes, items were found in a nearby disused mineshaft which cast a formidable light on the family's fate. Amongst assorted bones, charred, partially dissolved by acid, marked by sharp instruments and embedded with bullets, pieces of the military caps and belt buckles worn by Nicholas and his son were identified. Gradually, further evidence was amassed. It included fragments of a sapphire ring which the Tsar had never been able to remove from his finger, so closely did it fit, as well as a metal case in which he always carried Alexandra's portrait. Of Alexandra herself there remained an emerald cross – a gift from her mother-in-law – her spectacle-case, a fragment of her gown, one of a pair of pearl earrings that she always wore, a sapphire and diamond badge presented to her by her own Uhlan Guards, and a manicured finger which was assumed to be hers. Also exhumed were six women's metal corsets. Pierre Gilliard was sadly able to recognize a motley collection of nails, silver paper, coppers and a little lock as the contents of Alexis's pocket. Last to emerge from what was obviously a mass grave was the corpse of another spaniel, Jimmy, almost intact.

This physical evidence was later supplemented by the verbal testimony of eye-witnesses. The events of the fateful night of 16–17 July 1918 were finally reconstructed. On that night, the prisoners at the Ipatiev house, alternatively known as 'The House of Special Purpose', were woken up at midnight. They

OPPOSITE The imperial family on the roof of the house in Tobolsk where they were held prisoner from September 1917 to April 1918.

213

consisted of the Tsar, his wife and their five children, the faithful Dr Botkin, Alexandra's maid, Anna Demidova, the cook, Haritonov, and the valet, Alexis Trupp. They were told that Ekaterinburg was threatened by the White forces and that they must be ready to move elsewhere. An hour later, they were taken down to the basement. Nicholas, who was carrying Alexis, asked for chairs, which were brought. The Grand Duchesses tried to make their mother and brother comfortable with cushions.

It was in complete silence that the imperial party watched as seven armed men of a Cheka squad filed into the room and listened as Jacob Yurovsky, Bolshevik commandant of the Ipatiev house, brusquely informed the Tsar of the Russias that he must die. Nicholas barely had time to stammer 'What . . .?' when a blast from Yurovsky's revolver silenced him for ever. Burst after burst of gunfire from the whole squad filled the basement with blood and smoke. Where life remained, the men extinguished it with bayonet thrusts. At dawn, a dismal cavalcade of lorries bore the bodies of the last symbols of imperial Russia, wrapped in bloodstained sheets, to their gruesome grave.

A poignant picture of the last Tsar of Russia in captivity.

BIBLIOGRAPHY

Alexander, Grand Duke, *Once a Grand Duke*, New York 1932.

Baedeker, Karl, *Russia*, London 1914.

Baring, Maurice, *What I Saw in Russia*, London 1927.

Basily, Nicolas de, *Memoirs*, Stanford 1973.

Benckendorff, Count Constantine, *Half a Life*, London 1954.

Bill, Valentine T., *The Forgotten Class*, New York 1959.

Billington, James H., *The Icon and the Axe*, New York 1966.

Bruce-Lockhart, R. H., *Memoirs of a British Agent*, London 1974.

Buchanan, Sir George, *My Mission to Russia*, London 1923.

Buchanan, Meriel, *The Dissolution of an Empire*, London 1932.
　Ambassador's Daughter, London 1958.
　Petrograd, 1914–18, London 1918.

Buckle, Richard, *Nijinsky*, London 1971.

Buxhoeveden, Baroness Sophie, *The Life and Tragedy of Alexandra Feodorovna*, London 1928.

Cyril, Grand Duke, *My Life in Russia's Service*, London 1939.

Florinsky, T., *The End of the Russian Empire*, Yale 1931.

Frankel, Tobia, *The Russian Artist*, New York 1972.

Fülöp-Miller, René, *Rasputin, The Holy Devil*, London 1928.

Gilliard, Pierre, *Thirteen Years at the Russian Court*, London 1972.

Graham, Stephen, *The Way of Martha and the Way of Mary*, London 1915

Gregoriev, S. L., *The Diaghilev Ballet*, London 1953.

Karsavina, Tamara, *Theatre Street*, London 1948.

Kleinmichel, Countess Marie von Keller, *Memoirs of a Shipwrecked World*, New York 1923.

Kochan, Lionel, *Russia in Revolution*, London 1967.

Kokovtsov, Vladimir Nikolaevich, *Out of My Past*, Stanford 1935.

Kschessinska, Mathilde, *Dancing in St Petersburg*, London 1960.

Majolier, N., *Stepdaughter of Imperial Russia*, London 1940.

Marie Pavlovna, Grand Duchess, *Things I Remember*, London 1931.

Marye, George Thomas, *Nearing the End in Imperial Russia*, Philadelphia 1929.

Massie, Robert K., *Nicholas and Alexandra*, London 1968.

Mossolov, A. A., *At the Court of the Last Tsar*, London 1935.

Nemirovich-Danchenko, *My Life in the Russian Theatre*, London 1968.

Obolensky, Serge, *One Man in his Time*, New York 1958.
Paléologue, Maurice, *An Ambassador's Memoirs*, London 1973.
Paley, Princess, *Memories of Russia*, London 1924.
Pares, Sir Bernard, *My Russian Memories*, London 1931.
   The Fall of the Russian Monarchy, London and New York 1961.
Pasternak, Boris, *An Essay in Autobiography*, London 1959.
Rappoport, A. S., *Home Life in Russia*, London 1913.
Rodzianko, M. V., *The Reign of Rasputin*, London 1927.
Sazonov, Serge, *Fateful Years*, New York 1928.
Slonim, Marc, *Russian Theater*, London 1963.
Stanislavsky, Constantin, *My Life in Art*, London 1962.
Troyat, Henri, *Daily Life in Russia*, London 1961.
Vorres, Ian, *The Last Grand Duchess*, London 1964.
Vrubova, Anna, *Memories of the Russian Court*, London 1923.
Youssoupov, Prince Felix, *Lost Splendour*, London 1953.

ACKNOWLEDGMENTS

The author and publisher are grateful to the following individuals and agencies who have supplied illustrations. (Numbers refer to pages.)

8–9 Novosti Press Agency
11a Radio Times Hulton Picture Library
11b Mansell Collection
12 Victor Kennett
13 Radio Times Hulton Picture Library
14 John Massey Stewart
16 Novosti Press Agency
19 *Illustrated London News*
20–21 Novosti Press Agency
24 Victor Kennett
28 Radio Times Hulton Picture Library
30 Novosti Press Agency
30–31 Roger-Viollet
32–3 Mansell Collection
36–7 Victor Kennett
38 Mansell Collection
39 Snark International (Collection P. Peral)
40–41 Victor Kennett (courtesy of George Rainbird)
42 Radio Times Hulton Picture Library
45a Snark International (Collection P. Peral)
14b Roger-Viollet
46–7 Victor Kennett
50 Novosti Press Agency
51 Roger-Viollet
52–3, 56 Roger-Viollet
57, 58–9 John Massey Stewart

60 Mansell Collection (Archiv Henry Guttmann)
62–3, 65, 66, 68–9, 70 Novosti Press Agency
71, 72 *Illustrated London News*
75 Radio Times Hulton Picture Library
76, 78–9, 80, 84–5 Novosti Press Agency
87 John Massey Stewart
88a and b Novosti Press Agency
89 Mansell Collection
91 Roger-Viollet
92 Novosti Press Agency
93 Wiener Library
95 Novosti Press Agency
96–7 Sovfoto
99 Novosti Press Agency
100 Roger-Viollet
103 Radio Times Hulton Picture Library
104–5 Novosti Press Agency
106 Roger-Viollet
108–9 Desmond Tripp
111 Radio Times Hulton Picture Library
113 Sovfoto
115 Roger-Viollet
121 Mansell Collection
123 Weidenfeld and Nicolson Archive
124 Victoria and Albert Museum

126 Roger-Viollet
128 Weidenfeld and Nicolson
Archive
129 Radio Times Hulton
Picture Library
130 Weidenfeld and Nicolson
Archive
130–31 Mansell Collection
132 Victoria and Albert
Museum
133, 135 Weidenfeld and
Nicolson Archive
136 Snark International
138–9 Mansell Collection
141 Radio Times Hulton
Picture Library
142 John Massey Stewart
145 Radio Times Hulton
Picture Library
146 John Massey Stewart
149 Roger-Viollet
152 Radio Times Hulton
Picture Library
155 Roger-Viollet
160–61 Mansell Collection
163 Radio Times Hulton
Picture Library
166 Mansell Collection
168a and b, 170–71 Radio
Times Hulton Picture
Library
172, 175, 176 Mansell
Collection
178 Radio Times Hulton
Picture Library
180, 181 Mansell Collection
182–3 Roger-Viollet
184, 185 Radio Times Hulton
Picture Library
188–9 Novosti Press Agency
191 Mansell Collection
192, 195 Radio Times Hulton
Picture Library
198 Mansell Collection
199 Novosti Press Agency
203 Weidenfeld and Nicolson
Archive
206 Mansell Collection
207, 208–9 Sovfoto
209, 210 Novosti Press Agency
212, 214 Radio Times Hulton
Picture Library
endpapers John Massey
Stewart

Extracts from works still in copyright are reprinted by kind
permission of the following:
Jonathan Cape Ltd and the Executors of the Bernard Pares Estate,
for *The Fall of the Russian Monarchy* by Bernard Pares.
Hutchinson & Co. Ltd and Farrar, Straus & Giroux Inc., for *An
Ambassador's Memoirs* by Maurice Paléologue.

Picture research by Juliet Scott.

INDEX